BASKETBALL
CROSSWORDS

BASKETBALL CROSSWORDS

VOLUME 4

Dale Ratermann

MASTERS PRESS

NTC/Contemporary Publishing Group

Library of Congress Cataloging-in-Publication Data
is available from the United States Library of Congress.

Cover photograph copyright © 1997 Brian Spurlock

Published by Masters Press
A division of NTC/Contemporary Publishing Group, Inc.
4255 West Touhy Avenue, Lincolnwood (Chicago), Illinois 60646-1975 U.S.A.
Copyright © 1999 by Dale Ratermann
Printed in the United States of America
International Standard Book Number: 1-57028-214-5
International Standard Serial Number: 1521-5660
99 00 01 02 03 04 VL 19 18 17 16 15 14 13 12 11 10 9 8 7 6 5 4 3 2 1

For Nick and Beck

CONTENTS

BASKETBALL
CROSSWORDS

ATLANTA HAWKS

The Hawks' story is a matter of "What if?"

What if Red Auerbach had not been wooed away from coaching the Hawks to go to Boston where he led the Celtics to nine NBA titles as a coach and seven more as a general manager? And what if the same Red Auerbach hadn't orchestrated the trade which sent Celtics Ed Macauley and Cliff Hagan to the Hawks in exchange for the Hawks' first-round draft pick in 1956? That selection turned out to be Bill Russell.

It seems only appropriate that the Hawks' team color is red.

But despite those "what ifs," the Hawks enjoyed their finest period in the mid-1950s when they reached the NBA Finals four times in a five-year span, winning it all in 1958.

The Hawks were born in 1949–50 as the Tri-Cities Blackhawks. The NBA was only three years old and Tri-Cities was one of five expansion teams that season. The Blackhawks got off to a 1–6 start under Head Coach Roger Potter and a call was made to Auerbach who had coached the Washington Capitols to success in the previous three seasons. Auerbach took the helm and guided the Blackhawks to a 28–29 mark the rest of the way and a third place finish in the Western Division. But during the off-season, Auerbach was convinced to move to Boston by Celtics owner Walter Brown.

The Blackhawks played one more season in the Tri-Cities before moving to Milwaukee and shortening the nickname to "Hawks." The franchise stayed in Milwaukee for only four years. It was in Milwaukee, though, that the Hawks acquired one of the greatest players in NBA history—Bob Pettit.

The 6-foot-9 forward out of LSU didn't waste any time making an impact as a rookie in 1954–55. He averaged 20.4 points a game (which was the lowest of his career) and finished fourth in the league in scoring and third in rebounding, while being named to the all-star team. Before his career was over he was an 11-time all-star, two-time league MVP, four-time all-star game MVP, two-time scoring champion, and one-time rebounding leader. He was inducted into the Basketball Hall of Fame in 1970.

In 1955 the Hawks moved to St. Louis. They were just 33–39, but advanced to the Western Division finals before bowing out of the playoffs. After the playoffs, Auerbach made the fateful call from Boston which cost the Hawks a chance to have Russell in the same front line as Pettit.

In 1956–57, the Hawks improved by only one game in the regular season, but this time advanced to the NBA Finals, losing to the Celtics and their prized rookie, Russell, in a double-overtime seventh and deciding game. In 1957–58, the Hawks improved to 41–31 and avenged their previous playoff loss to the Celtics by beating Boston in the Finals, 4–2.

The Hawks made it to the Finals twice more in the next three years. They won the Western Division in 1958–59 with a 49–23 record, but were beaten in the Division finals by Minneapolis. In 1959–60, they not only won the division, but extended the Celtics to seven games before losing the title. And in 1960–61, they won the division for the fifth straight year, but were beaten by the arch-rival Celtics in the Finals, 4–1.

A slow decline in wins followed over the ensuing seasons. In 1967–68, the Hawks went 56–26 and won the Western Division. That team featured Zelmo Beatty, Lenny Wilkens, Joe Caldwell, Paul Silas, Bill Bridges and Lou Hudson. But the Hawks were eliminated by San Francisco in the first round of the playoffs. Interest in St. Louis waned and the franchise moved to Atlanta.

The Hawks floundered as a mediocre team for the next decade until Ted Turner purchased the franchise in 1977. Three years later the Hawks won a division title, but plummeted the following year. Mike Fratello was hired as the head coach in 1983 and lifted the Hawks to a franchise record 57 wins in 1986–87, but Atlanta lost in the second round of the playoffs.

Throughout the 1980s, the dominant player for the Hawks was Dominique Wilkins. The nine-time all-star led the NBA in scoring in 1985–86 and amassed more than 25,000 career points.

Fratello was out following the 1989–90 season and Bob Weiss was named the new coach. The Hawks remained competitive, going 43–39 in 1990–91, 38–44 in an injury-plagued 1991–92 and 43–39 in 1992–93, but Weiss was fired when the Hawks couldn't advance past the first round of the playoffs, a problem that plagued the Hawks every year but four times since from 1970 to '93.

Lenny Wilkens, the former all-star for the Hawks, was named head coach (the Hawks' 24th) in the summer of 1993. He turned around Atlanta's fortunes immediately. The Hawks went 57–25 in 1993–94 en route to a division title and the best record in the Eastern Conference. But they stumbled in the second round of the playoffs. They slipped to 42 wins in 1994–95, but Wilkens made history by breaking Auerbach's NBA record for most career coaching victories (938).

The Hawks rebounded with 46 victories in 1995–96 and upset Indiana in the first round of the playoffs. Atlanta won 56 games in 1996–97 and 50 in 1997–98. However, the Hawks were beaten in the second round of the playoffs for the fourth time in five seasons.

Christian Laettner was a member of the original Dream Team in 1992.

INDIVIDUAL RECORDS

Career

Points: 23,292, Dominique Wilkins, 1982–94

Rebounds: 12,851, Bob Pettit, 1954–65

Assists: 3,866, Glenn Rivers, 1983–91

Field Goal Pct.: .553, Mike Glenn, 1981–85

Free Throw Pct.: .844, Steve Smith, 1994–98

Season

Points: 2,429, Bob Pettit, 1961–62

Rebounds: 1,540, Bob Pettit, 1960–61

Assists: 823, Glenn Rivers, 1986–87

Field Goal Pct.: .588, Mike Glenn, 1984–85

Free Throw Pct.: .891, Tom McMillen, 1978–79

ACROSS

2. A cheer
4. Wager on a game
6. Dunk
8. Court
9. The Big Z
11. Official
13. Averaged 12.7 reb. a game from 1962–71
15. Publicity (init.)
16. Noise at end of period
18. Contests
20. Blackman's nickname
21. Take the ball away (abbr.)
22. The Human Highlight Film

23. Set NBA record with 14 turn-overs in '78 game
24. Painted area of floor around the basket
25. Floating billboards
27. Hawks, Hornets or Celtics
31. Former
32. Hawks' career rebounding leader and family
35. Tied NBA record with 7 3-pointers in 1 quarter in '97
37. Spud
38. ___-announcer (init.)
40. ___ Pellom
41. Part of FTA
43. Only player in NCAA history to

record more than 200 assists and 100 steals in back-to-back seasons

45. Metal baskets

47. Star of the game

49. Night before the game

50. Carom at own basket (init.)

52. Wire service (init.)

53. Taps

55. Super Lou

57. Jim Davis' alma mater (init.)

58. Tally

59. Bill Bridges' alma mater (init.)

60. Kentucky star earned Hall of Fame honors in St. Louis

DOWN

1. Red, yellow or blue

2. Hold

3. NBA's Most Improved Player in '98

4. No games scheduled

5. Deadlock

6. Bracey, Henson or Hawes

7. Arena sign

8. Fisticuffs

10. Wayne Rollins' nickname

12. Very mad

14. Modes of distribution for play-by-play broadcasts

17. Falcons' league (init.)

18. Michigan's Rickey

19. Before Cormick, Elroy or Millen

21. Ken Norman's nickname

22. NBA's winningest coach

23. Glenn Rivers' nickname

24. Christian

26. 3-time NBA Defensive Player of the Year

28. Roster spot for hurt players (init.)

29. Former home of the Kings (init.)

30. Against (abbr.)

33. Pick up the tab

34. Stomach muscle (abbr.)

36. Pistol Pete

37. Had 1,258 reb. in 1991–92, most ever by an Atlanta Hawk

39. Pass leading to a basket

42. Jump, hook and set

44. Bang off the rim

46. 3-pointer in Rome

48. Where severely injured players are sent (init.)

51. Dean "___ Dream" Meminger

53. Plastic tip of a shoelace

54. Go ___ guy

56. ___ or die

Solution on page 176

RETIRED UNIFORM NUMBERS

9	Bob Pettit
23	Lou Hudson

```
N  O  B  M  O  T  U  M  L  T  I  T  T  E  P
L  W  U  O  L  L  E  T  A  R  F  W  D  E  C
O  N  O  M  G  M  B  S  L  U  I  I  H  S  A
V  A  M  R  B  A  O  E  N  L  O  L  I  I  L
E  A  G  R  B  R  E  U  A  I  O  L  E  N  D
L  A  U  H  I  T  H  E  M  T  K  I  V  O  W
L  S  E  G  D  I  R  B  B  N  Y  S  W  S  E
E  I  R  S  V  N  E  O  V  O  U  E  H  R  L
T  S  I  E  R  I  V  E  R  S  R  D  A  E  L
T  N  N  L  I  U  S  L  N  D  E  R  G  D  E
E  I  L  V  E  M  E  E  A  U  M  S  A  N  R
N  K  E  Y  I  V  K  L  E  H  D  L  N  E  N
H  L  I  T  O  L  A  E  T  T  N  E  R  H  N
D  I  H  L  I  Y  L  H  C  I  V  A  R  A  M
R  W  L  W  B  L  A  Y  L  O  C  K  I  R  B
```

BEATY	GUERIN	MUTOMBO
BLAYLOCK	HAGAN	PETTIT
BRIDGES	HENDERSON	RIVERS
BROWN	HUDSON	SELVY
CALDWELL	LAETTNER	SMITH
DREW	LOVELLETTE	WILKENS
EHLO	MARAVICH	WILKINS
FRATELLO	MARTIN	WILLIS

BOSTON CELTICS

When the great teams of any professional sports league are discussed, few can approach the Celtics' dominance. There are the New York Yankees. The Montreal Canadiens. The Green Bay Packers. And the Celtics.

The Celtics have won better than 60 percent of their games and 16 NBA titles, including an incredible eight in a row from 1959–66. And six other times they won at least 60 games in a season without winning the championship.

Maybe that's why the Celtics are one of only two teams from the original 11 NBA franchises that hasn't disbanded or moved. (The New York Knicks are the other team.)

There was nothing special about the Celtics when they began play in 1946. They were coached by John "Honey" Russell, led in scoring by Connie Simmons (10.3 points a game) and finished in a tie for last place in the Eastern Division at 22–38. The following three seasons weren't much better.

But then owner Walter Brown decided it would take a unique person, one of ingenuity and determination, to steer the fortunes of his club. He convinced Red Auerbach to leave the Tri-Cities Blackhawks and become the Celtics' head coach. Auerbach has been a part of the Celtics ever since.

In 1950–51, he guided Boston to a 39–30 record in his first season and averaged 40 wins in his first six years. But on Apr. 29, 1956, Auerbach devised a trade that made the Celtics a dynasty. Auerbach traded Ed Macauley (a six-time all-star still in his prime) and Cliff Hagan (a future Hall of Famer) to St. Louis for the Hawks' first-round draft pick. Dicey? That pick was Bill Russell. The 6-foot-10 center out of the University of San Francisco made the swap pay off in a hurry, leading the Celtics to an NBA title in his rookie season. The Celtics lost to St. Louis in the championship series the following year, but then ran off eight consecutive titles. They skipped a year, then won two more championships. That completed a run of 11 championships in a 13-year span. Russell didn't do it single-handedly. He had an excellent supporting cast, including Bob Cousy, Bill Sharman and Sam Jones.

But the dynasty didn't end with Auerbach's move into the front office in the summer of 1966 or Russell's retirement following the 1968–69 season. They won two more titles in the 1970s and three in the 1980s.

Tom Heinsohn coached Boston to championships in 1973–74 and 1975–76. The stars of those squads were John Havlicek, Dave Cowens, Jo Jo White and Paul Silas.

Bill Fitch was the head coach in 1980–81 when Larry Bird guided the Celtics to the first of his three NBA titles. K. C. Jones was at the helm for the 1983–84 and 1985–86 championships. Assisting Bird were Robert Parish, Kevin McHale and Dennis Johnson.

Boston made it to the Finals again in 1986–87 (losing to the Lakers), but it hasn't been back. Jones was replaced as coach by Jimmy Rodgers in 1988, but when the Celtics failed to get past the first round of the playoffs, he was replaced two years later by Chris Ford. The Celtics advanced to the second round in 1990–91 and 1991–92, but were beaten in the first round by Charlotte in 1992–93.

The Celtics fell to 32 wins and failed to qualify for the playoffs in 1993–94. Despite getting into post-season play the following year, Ford was released when the team won just 35 games. M. L. Carr, the Celtics' director of basketball operations, named himself the head coach for the 1995–96 season.

Boston finished 33–49, but the season was exciting, nonetheless. The Celtics moved into the $160 million, 18,600-seat FleetCenter after playing their previous 49 seasons in the famed Boston Garden. The Celtics won better than 75 percent of their games on the fabled parquet floor, which was first used in 1946. The 247 5-foot-square panels were resurfaced and transported to the new FleetCenter.

The Celtics' performance on the new floor has suffered. Boston fell to a franchise-worst 15–67 in 1996–97. Carr was relieved of his duties and Rick Pitino was lured from the University of Kentucky. Pitino was given complete control of the franchise (although Auerbach maintains the title of Vice Chairman of the Board).

He completely revamped the roster. During the 1997–98 season, the Celtics used 19 players en route to a 36–46 record. Then with the 10th pick in the 1998 draft, the Celtics selected Kansas forward Paul Pierce.

Despite all the highs, the Celtics franchise was struck with tragedy twice in recent years. Following the 1986 draft, the Celtics' No. 1 pick (and second selection overall), Maryland's Len Bias, died of a drug overdose. Then in the summer of 1993, all-star guard Reggie Lewis collapsed and died while shooting around.

Copyright © 1997 Brian Spurlock/Spurlock Photography, Inc.

Antoine Walker led the Celtics with 22.4 points per game in 1997–98.

INDIVIDUAL RECORDS

Career

> Points: 26,395, John Havlicek, 1962–78
> Rebounds: 21,620, Bill Russell, 1956–69
> Assists: 6,945, Bob Cousy, 1950–63
> Field Goal Pct.: .559, Cedric Maxwell, 1977–85
> Free Throw Pct.: .886, Larry Bird, 1979–92

Season

> Points: 2,338, John Havlicek, 1970–71
> Rebounds: 1,930, Bill Russell, 1963–64
> Assists: 715, Bob Cousy, 1959–60
> Field Goal Pct.: .609, Cedric Maxwell, 1979–80
> Free Throw Pct.: .932, Bill Sharman, 1958–59

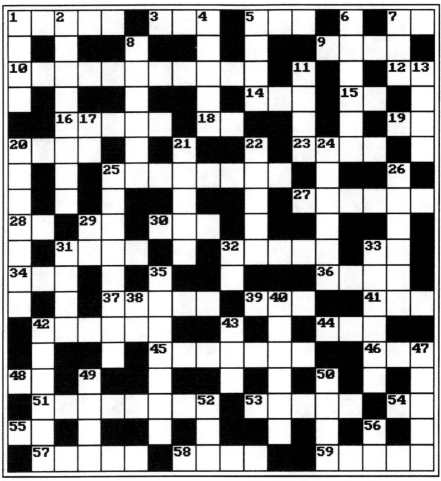

ACROSS

1. Tiny
3. Hang onto to the ball
5. Trick defense: ___-and-1
7. Arena sign
9. 1st round pick casualty
10. Celtics' home
12. Brad Lohaus' alma mater (init.)
14. DeCovan Kadell Brown's nickname
15. Roster spot for hurt players (init.)
16. Fast___
18. Take away the ball (abbr.)
19. Play ___ or trade me!
20. Boast
23. Location on the floor
25. Player turned coach turned broadcaster
27. Swaps
28. On the back of a uniform (abbr.)
29. Chauncey Billups' uniform number in Rome
30. Wager on a game
31. Tug
32. All-star guard who died during workout
33. Rejection (init.)
34. Expected time of touchdown (init.)
36. Star of the game
37. Celtics' career assists leader

39. Ref's relative
41. Sign a contract
42. Slang for basketball players
44. NBA's TV network
45. His No. 21 is retired
46. Trainer's equipment: medicine ___
48. ___-announcer (init.)
51. Easy Ed
53. K.C. or Sam
54. TV talk: ___, Mom!
55. ___ and in
57. Device used for multiple autographs
58. Winner of '72 basketball Olympic gold medal (init.)
59. Dribble hard to the basket

DOWN

1. Secure
2. Red
4. Entrances to the arena
5. The Hick from French Lick
6. Celtics' head coach
7. Alton Lister's alma mater (init.)
8. No. 32 became GM of Timberwolves
11. Basket cords

13. Treats a sprained ankle
17. Michigan guard played for Celtics in 1991–92 (init.)
20. Dribbles the ball
21. Sign above entrance
22. Jo Jo
24. Double zero
25. Celtics' career scoring leader
26. No. 19 is now head coach of the Mavericks
29. Quinn Buckner's alma mater (init.)
31. Slang for father
32. Playoff nemesis (init.)
33. Errant shots
35. Celtics' career rebounding leader
38. Do ___ die
40. Ex-NBA scoring champ played for Celtics in 1978–79
42. Titleists
43. 3-point line
47. Tickle the ___
49. Collegiate governing body (init.)
50. Are ahead
52. Marv Albert's call
56. Bill Russell's uniform number in Rome

Solution on page 176

RETIRED UNIFORM NUMBERS

00	Robert Parish	18	Dave Cowens
1	Walter Brown	18	Jim Loscutoff
2	Red Auerbach	19	Don Nelson
3	Dennis Johnson	21	Bill Sharman
6	Bill Russell	22	Ed Macauley
10	Jo Jo White	23	Frank Ramsey
14	Bob Cousy	24	Sam Jones
15	Tom Heinsohn	25	K. C. Jones
16	Satch Sanders	32	Kevin McHale
17	John Havlicek	33	Larry Bird
		35	Reggie Lewis

```
N  A  M  R  A  H  S  R  U  S  S  E  L  L  H
S  A  N  D  E  R  S  L  S  O  N  H  E  C  P
A  C  E  O  R  A  H  K  E  C  I  L  V  A  H
M  O  M  A  X  W  E  L  L  V  A  L  R  A  M
R  W  W  N  C  S  R  S  L  D  E  I  E  H  A
A  E  A  H  S  A  E  I  K  S  S  Y  W  C  C
H  N  C  I  I  S  R  N  S  H  S  I  X  A  A
S  S  O  C  A  T  I  R  O  U  S  H  A  B  U
N  P  U  N  D  T  E  W  O  J  A  B  M  R  L
O  A  S  R  W  O  L  C  E  B  I  O  O  E  E
S  R  I  E  G  O  O  W  O  L  B  S  N  U  Y
N  B  U  W  E  N  R  L  C  R  E  K  L  A  W
H  R  A  M  S  E  Y  B  J  E  L  A  H  C  M
O  H  O  H  H  E  I  N  S  O  H  N  C  H  Y
J  P  I  T  I  N  O  H  A  N  O  S  L  E  N
```

AUERBACH	HEINSOHN	PARISH
BIAS	JOHNSON	PITINO
BIRD	JONES	RAMSEY
BROWN	LEWIS	RUSSELL
CARR	MACAULEY	SANDERS
COUSY	MAXWELL	SHARMAN
COWENS	MCHALE	WALKER
HAVLICEK	NELSON	WHITE

CHARLOTTE HORNETS

An NBA franchise in Charlotte? Charlotte, N.C.? You gotta be kidding.

That had to be the reaction around the nation when Charlotte businessman George Shinn expressed an interest in 1985 to land one of four NBA expansion teams. But it was no joke when on April Fool's Day, 1987, the NBA informed Shinn and the city that they indeed would be joining the NBA. The induction cost Shinn and his partners $32.5 million.

There's no doubting the city now. The Hornets have led the league in home attendance in seven of their eight seasons and have sold out 317 consecutive home games. They boast eight of the top 10 season attendance totals in NBA history and have sold out all 41 home dates for seven straight years. As for merchandise, the Hornets' teal T-shirts, jerseys and hats, peaked as the league's leader in licensed product sales during the 1995–96 season. That's off the court. On the court, it's a different story for expansion teams, right? Wrong.

The Hornets did start slowly, though. As a matter of fact, they weren't even sure that was going to be the nickname. A contest was held in November, 1986, to name the team and "Spirit" was the pick out of more than 8,000 entries. But then in June, 1987, when the franchise was official, another contest was held and "Hornets" was the winner. The name Hornets has historical significance for the Charlotte area, going back to the American Revolution. As local lore has it, British General Charles Cornwallis declared after an American uprising, "There's a rebel behind every bush. It's a veritable nest of hornets." In addition, for many years there was a minor league baseball team and later a World Football League team in Charlotte called the Hornets.

Carl Scheer was named the general manager and Dick Harter was hired as the first head coach. The assistant coaches were Ed Badger and Gene Littles. The expansion draft of NBA cast-offs and wannabes gave the Hornets the rights to unknowns such as Sedric Toney, Clinton Wheeler and Bernard Thompson. But they were able to acquire usable veterans Dell Curry, Muggsy Bogues, Rickey Green, Dave Hoppen, Michael Holton and Ralph Lewis. Their first college draft also produced Rex Chapman.

The Hornets made the decision to try to win immediately and signed as many seasoned veterans as were available. Among the free agents they lured to North Carolina were Kurt Rambis and Earl Cureton. They also made trades to acquire veterans Kelly Tripucka and Robert Reid.

The first game in the franchise's history was Nov. 4, 1988 vs. the Cleveland Cavaliers. The starting line-up was: Tripucka, Rambis, Hoppen, Green and

Reid. The first shot was taken by Green, but the first points were scored by Tripucka. Charlotte lost its opener, 133–93. The first win came against the Los Angeles Clippers in Game 3, and the Hornets struggled to a 20–62 record.

The 1989–90 squad added J.R. Reid in the draft, but fell to 19–63 and Harter was replaced midway through the season by Littles. In 1990–91, Kendall Gill was selected in the draft and they improved to 26–56. By virtue of that record, and a little luck in the draft lottery, the Hornets wound up with the No. 1 pick in the 1991 college draft. With that selection, they chose the college player of the year, UNLV's Larry Johnson.

Allan Bristow was named head coach prior to the 1991–92 season and helped lead the Hornets to a 31–51 record. Johnson was the consensus NBA Rookie of the Year, averaging 19.2 points and 11.0 rebounds.

The Hornets had the No. 2 selection in the 1992 college draft and plucked Georgetown's Alonzo Mourning. That set the stage for a 1992–93 season that won't soon be forgotten in Charlotte.

Those that thought Johnson's numbers as a rookie were good, were impressed even more by Mourning. The 6-foot-10 center averaged 21.0 points, 10.3 rebounds and 3.47 blocked shots a game. Yet, he didn't win the NBA Rookie of the Year award. (Shaquille O'Neal did.) And Johnson showed his rookie season was no fluke, improving to 22.1 points a game and being named to the Eastern Conference's all-star team. That pair led the Hornets to a 44–38 record, third place in the Central Division and a spot in the 1993 playoffs.

The Hornets faced the fabled Boston Celtics in the first round and upset the higher-seeded Celtics, 3 games to 1, to become the first of the most recent expansion squads to have a winning record and the first to advance in the playoffs. The Hornets were eliminated in the second round by the Atlantic Division champion New York Knicks, 4–1.

With Johnson out with injuries for 31 games and Mourning out for 22, the Hornets slipped to a 41–41 record in 1993–94 and missed the playoffs. But with healthy bodies the following season, Charlotte went 50–32 and finished second in the Central Division. But the fourth-seeded Hornets were eliminated in the first round of the playoffs by the recently-returned Michael Jordan and the Chicago Bulls, 3 games to 1.

Prior to the 1995–96 season, Mourning was traded to Miami. The key player the Hornets got in return, Glen Rice, led Charlotte in scoring (21.6 points per game), to go with Johnson's 20.5 points and 8.4 rebounds per game. But Charlotte fell to 41–41 and were five wins short of making the playoffs.

Bristow was relieved of his coaching duties following the season and replaced by Dave Cowens, a hall of fame performer for Boston. A short time later, Johnson was traded to New York in exchange for Anthony Mason and Brad Lohaus.

The changes paid immediate dividends. Mason became the team's best all-around player; Rice increased his scoring to 26.8 points per game; and Cowens led the Hornets to a club-record 54 wins. The Hornets, however, were swept in the first round of the playoffs by the Knicks.

Charlotte won 51 games in 1997–98 and were again led by Mason and Rice. The Hornets beat the Atlanta Hawks in the first round of the playoffs, 3 games to 1, before bowing out in the second round to the eventual NBA champion, Chicago, 4 games to 1.

Glen Rice was the MVP of the 1997 NBA All-Star Game.

INDIVIDUAL RECORDS
Career

Points: 9,839, Dell Curry, 1988–98

Rebounds: 3,479, Larry Johnson, 1991–96

Assists: 5,557, Muggsy Bogues, 1988–98

Field Goal Pct.: .529, Kenny Gattison, 1989–95

Free Throw Pct.: .879, Kelly Tripucka, 1988–91

Season

Points: 2,115, Glen Rice, 1996–97

Rebounds: 899, Larry Johnson, 1991–92

Assists: 867, Muggsy Bogues, 1989–90

Field Goal Pct.: .564, Dave Hoppen, 1988–89

Free Throw Pct.: .910, Kelly Tripucka, 1990–91

ACROSS

3. Hornets' career rebounding leader
7. Show the action again on TV
10. Signals the end of a period
12. Charlotte's not a city, but a big ___.
14. Type of defense
15. Hornets' leading scorer in debut season
17. Former Knick claims to own more movies than Blockbuster
18. ___ Reid
19. Double-team
20. Scott Haffner's alma mater (init.)
21. FGM divided by FGA
22. Fastbreaks
23. Do ___ die
24. Ref's relative
25. Coach: ___ way or the highway.
26. Kept on the scoreboard (abbr.)
29. ___ and in
31. Carom at opponent's basket (init.)
34. Bespectacled forward from Santa Clara
36. Take the ball away (abbr.)
38. Muggsy Bogues' position (init.)
40. Stadium
41. Ahead: ___ top

43. Arena sign
45. Hornets' career assists leader
46. Away
47. His Yugoslavian wedding was televised in his native homeland
48. Former
50. Column heading on roster (abbr.)
52. Rejection (init.)
53. Years since births
54. There are 3 on the court for jump balls
57. George Zidek's alma mater (init.)
59. Baseball stat (init.)
61. Low post position
63. Jerseys and shorts
67. Rex Chapman's alma mater (init.)
68. Basket cord
69. Extra period (abbr.)
70. Aide
71. Foot and ankle coverings

DOWN

1. Tried to score
2. Publicity (init.)
4. Bradley guard started 164 consecutive games from 1993–95
5. Rode the pine
6. Richmond guard traded to N.J. for Rumeal Robinson
7. Blackman's nickname
8. Mode of team travel
9. Season

11. Hornets' career scoring leader
13. Afternoon rest
14. Hornets' No. 1 pick in '92 draft
16. National spokesman for Nautica Sports apparel
18. Leaps
24. Tom Chambers' alma mater (init.)
25. Type of x ray (init.)
27. Swap
28. Glen Rice's alma mater (init.)
30. Wire service (init.)
32. ___-announcer (init.)
33. Area for subs
35. Record holders
37. Throw the ball away (abbr.)
39. Hornets' career field goal pct. leader
42. Owns and operates record label MG 20/20
44. Illinois guard had 2 triple-doubles in '95
49. Pass leading to a basket
51. Spin
52. Game sphere
55. ___-captain
56. Dunk
58. Go in reverse
60. Tosses an alley-oop pass
62. Down and ___
63. Joe Wolf's alma mater (init.)
64. Longtime U.S. Olympic basketball coach
65. Rest on the bench
66. Spectator
68. NBA's TV network

Solution on page 177

RETIRED UNIFORM NUMBERS

1   Sixth Man (fans)

```
A  B  K  S  L  N  N  O  S  I  T  T  A  G  B
M  T  H  A  W  K  I  N  S  C  U  N  M  U  O
I  R  D  G  M  E  T  B  U  R  R  E  L  L  G
B  I  U  E  I  D  D  R  A  M  B  I  S  I  U
M  P  T  R  R  L  E  L  G  H  Y  E  C  T  E
A  U  R  R  N  T  L  R  D  E  O  U  R  T  S
R  C  G  E  O  I  E  I  N  I  R  J  I  L  I
I  K  N  N  I  E  N  N  A  R  V  E  I  E  L
K  A  I  O  N  D  O  G  Y  M  L  A  R  S  N
S  S  N  I  S  S  P  E  A  N  E  L  C  T  A
N  I  R  O  N  I  C  S  K  V  A  T  I  R  M
E  I  U  H  R  I  O  O  A  A  K  M  O  G  P
W  N  O  I  R  N  I  W  O  T  S  I  R  B  A
O  J  M  G  E  I  G  E  R  Y  W  E  S  E  H
C  H  A  R  T  E  R  C  N  A  M  W  E  N  C
```

BOGUES	GATTISON	LITTLES
BRISTOW	GEIGER	MASON
BURRELL	GILL	MOURNING
CHAPMAN	GILLIAM	NEWMAN
COWENS	GREEN	RAMBIS
CURETON	HARTER	REID
CURRY	HAWKINS	RICE
DIVAC	JOHNSON	TRIPUCKA

CHICAGO BULLS

It was being billed as "Repeat Three-peat." Could the Chicago Bulls win a third consecutive NBA title for the second time in eight seasons? Is it something another franchise can accomplish in the next decade? Will the Bulls be broken up or make a run at another championship?

The answers to those questions are: Yes, probably not, and we'll see.

When the Bulls were born in 1966–67, no one envisioned what would happen in the 1990s. No one could predict the emergence of the greatest player in history, Michael Jordan. No one could foresee laser light shows and pulsating player introductions. And no one could portend standing room only crowds night after night in Chicago Stadium or the new United Center.

Not when only 4,772 people showed up on an average night in that first season, even though the Bulls set an expansion team record with 33 wins. John "Red" Kerr was named the NBA Coach of the Year when the Bulls stunned the NBA by qualifying for the playoffs. The first four seasons showed gradual progress. By 1970–71, the Bulls, then under Coach Dick Motta, won 51 games. That was followed by 57, 51, 54 and 47-win seasons. But then the bottom dropped out. The Bulls won only 24 games in 1975–76 and qualified for the playoffs only twice in a nine-year period. They went 27–55 in 1983–84 under Coach Kevin Loughery. That record put the Bulls in the No. 3 position for the 1984 college draft.

Houston had the first pick and selected (H)akeem Olajuwon out of the University of Houston. Portland had the second pick and opted for Sam Bowie of Kentucky. That left the Bulls, who had to decide among a sophomore out of the University of North Carolina, Michael Jordan, his UNC teammate Sam Perkins or Auburn's Charles Barkley. Chicago took Jordan. The rest, as they say, is history.

In Jordan's rookie season of 1984–85, he averaged 28.2 points, 6.5 rebounds, 5.9 assists and 2.39 steals a game. He was an all-star and the Rookie of the Year. But the Bulls were only 38–44 and sold out just seven home games. Loughery was replaced by Stan Albeck and the Bulls stumbled to a 30–52 record as Jordan missed all but 18 games with a broken navicular tarsal bone in his left foot. Albeck was replaced by Doug Collins and Jordan began to take charge. He led the NBA in scoring with 37.1 points per game (his first of seven consecutive scoring titles) and the Bulls went 40–42. In 1987–88 they improved to 50–32 and advanced to the second round of the playoffs. The following season, they went 47–35, but made it to the Eastern Conference finals before losing to the eventual champion Detroit Pistons.

Phil Jackson took over as head coach for the 1989–90 season. The Bulls improved again, this time to 55–27, but again were defeated by the Pistons in the Conference finals. They got out of the gate slowly in 1990–91, going 12–8. They went 49–13 the rest of the way. The Bulls swept the New York Knicks in the first round, 3 games to none. They beat Philadelphia, 4–1, then avenged their earlier defeats at the hands of the Pistons by sweeping them in the Conference finals, 4–0. That set the stage for their first NBA Finals. The foe? Magic Johnson and the Los Angeles Lakers.

The Lakers won the opening game of the series in Chicago Stadium. But the Bulls won the next game, then swept three games in L.A. to win the championship. The following season, talk of the Bulls repeating became reality when they rolled to a 67–15 record. They won the opening round playoff series over Miami, 3–0, and were forced to seven games by the Knicks in the second round. But after a 4–2 win in the Conference finals over Cleveland, the Bulls were ready for the Portland Trail Blazers in the Finals. Jordan and the Bulls answered the challenges from Clyde Drexler and the Trail Blazers, winning their second title, 4–2.

What was left to prove? How about three in a row? Only the Minneapolis Lakers (1952–54) and Celtics (1959–65) had managed to win as many as three titles in a row. The Bulls went 57–25 and breezed through the first round of the playoffs, beating Atlanta, 3–0. They swept Cleveland in the second round, 4–0. They were slowed, but not stopped, by the Knicks in the Conference finals, 4–2. That set up a title match vs. the Phoenix Suns and Charles Barkley. Final: Bulls 4, Suns 2.

Jordan shocked the world when he announced his retirement (and subsequent foray into professional baseball) prior to the 1993–94 season. The Bulls still managed to win 55 games, behind all-star Scottie Pippen, but were bounced out of the playoffs in the second round.

Then in 1994–95 the Bulls were off to a 34–31 start when Jordan returned, with as much fanfare as when he announced his premature retirement. Chicago went 13–4 the rest of the way, but fell in the playoffs in the second round to the Orlando Magic, 4 games to 2.

That set the stage for the 1995–96 season. The Bulls started 5–0. They were 23–2 on Christmas Day and talk began of just how remarkable the season could be. Could they match the Lakers' record 69 wins of 1971–72? Could they win 70? They followed their third loss with 18 consecutive victories to stand 41–3. Then came a human-like two-game losing streak. But the Bulls won 31 of their final 36 games to finish 72–10. Jordan led the league in scoring with 30.4 points per game. Newcomer Dennis Rodman led the league in rebounding with an average of 14.9. Jordan was the league MVP, Jackson the Coach of the Year.

In the playoffs, the Bulls rolled past Miami, 3–0, and New York, 4–1. Then came a rematch with Orlando. The Bulls blasted the Magic, 4-zip. In the Finals, the Bulls cruised to a 3 games to none lead, then beat Seattle, 4–2, to cap a season that may never be matched.

Chicago came close the following year of matching that glorious season. The Bulls won 69 games and rolled to the championship, losing just four playoff games, including two in the Finals to the Utah Jazz.

What was left for an encore? Three in a row—again. The Bulls were hit by injuries, yet still managed to finish 62–20, but this time they relinquished home court advantage in the Finals to the revengeful Jazz. It didn't matter. Chicago won again in six games.

Phil Jackson lived up to his preseason promise of leaving the team at year's end. As the lockout in the NBA grew longer in the summer of 1998, no one knew the answer as to whether or not Jordan, Pippen and Rodman would return for another shot at a title.

Michael Jordan is a five-time league MVP.

INDIVIDUAL RECORDS

Career

Points: 29,277, Michael Jordan, 1984–93, 1995–98

Rebounds: 5,845, Michael Jordan, 1984–93, 1995–98

Assists: 5,012, Michael Jordan, 1984–93, 1995–98

Field Goal Pct.: .587, Artis Gilmore, 1976–82, 1987–88

Free Throw Pct.: .900, Craig Hodges, 1988–92

Season

Points: 3,041, Michael Jordan, 1986–87

Rebounds: 1,133, Tom Boerwinkle, 1970–71

Assists: 908, Guy Rodgers, 1966–67

Field Goal Pct.: .670, Artis Gilmore, 1980–81

Free Throw Pct.: .935, Ricky Sobers, 1980–81

ACROSS

3. Column heading on ticket
5. Horace and Harvey
9. Fast___
11. Arena signs
13. FGM divided by FGA
14. Orlando
16. Yell
17. Expected time of touchdown (init.)
18. Carom at own basket (init.)
19. Each player gets 6 a game (init.)
22. Extra period (abbr.)
23. Away

27. Breakfast drink (init.)
30. No. 4 now is a rival coach
32. Bulls' home
33. Child
34. Tate Armstrong's alma mater (init.)
36. ___-___ record (init.)
37. Bradley forward was a 4-time all-star in the '70s
40. Opponents
41. Card game
43. Did sprints
44. Fastbreak
45. Swaps
49. Shoots wide

51. Night before a game
52. Before down or after put
54. Bulls GM who drafted Jordan
56. Rotate
57. A quarter
58. ___-announcer (init.)
61. Chef
62. Elbow or knee protection
63. Low post position

DOWN

1. NBA's TV network
2. Jerry Sloan's alma mater (init.)
4. Time out drink
6. After locker or training
7. Series of road games
8. Set Bulls record with 1,133 rebounds in 1970–71
10. Stadium
12. Cross trained in a pool
13. Warm-up: ___-game routine
15. ___ to guy
16. Change direction sharply
20. 1-handed play signal
21. Place on the floor
24. UNLV guard was an all-rookie team pick in '79

25. Bulls coach for 6 titles
26. St. Francis defensive stalwart was a 3-time all-star
28. Hit .202 as a minor-league baseball player
29. Author of a children's book, "Reach Higher"
31. Bulls' leading scorer from 1970 through '76
32. Jersey and shorts
35. Rodney McCray's alma mater (init.)
38. Won 3-point contest at '97 all-star weekend
39. The Worm
41. Throws the ball
42. Regulations
46. Pass leading to a basket
47. Quarter
48. Older players
50. Roster spot for hurt players (init.)
52. Errant shot
53. Boots
55. Points ___ turnovers
59. Stomach muscle (abbr.)
60. A cheer

Solution on page 177

RETIRED UNIFORM NUMBERS

4	Jerry Sloan
10	Bob Love
23	Michael Jordan

```
C  B  L  Y  A  R  M  E  R  O  M  L  I  G  P
W  P  R  C  O  L  L  I  N  S  M  O  A  I  H
O  W  A  O  N  Y  R  B  L  O  A  R  P  N  A
O  A  E  G  W  R  O  O  T  C  M  P  T  O  R
L  F  L  L  E  N  V  T  C  S  E  H  L  S  P
R  N  K  K  Z  E  A  O  T  N  E  S  X  X  E
I  A  N  E  L  S  K  R  O  U  D  U  O  A  R
D  A  I  G  T  U  O  R  S  R  A  T  P  P  O
G  E  W  D  K  N  Z  M  N  L  R  D  E  O  D
E  N  R  I  G  I  K  R  A  E  O  Z  R  I  G
O  A  E  R  O  U  E  J  M  S  K  A  N  O  E
O  D  O  L  O  G  O  L  D  U  L  J  N  G  R
N  R  B  Y  E  L  G  N  O  L  A  V  O  U  S
I  O  R  E  K  L  A  W  R  E  I  L  N  A  V
W  J  A  C  K  S  O  N  N  T  G  R  A  N  T
```

ARMSTRONG	JORDAN	RAY
BOERWINKLE	KERR	RODGERS
BROWN	KUKOC	RODMAN
COLLINS	LONGLEY	SLOAN
GILMORE	LOVE	THEUS
GRANT	MOTTA	VAN LIER
HARPER	PAXSON	WALKER
JACKSON	PIPPEN	WOOLRIDGE

CLEVELAND CAVALIERS

If the most recent expansion teams in the NBA thought they had it bad, maybe they should take a look at the Cavaliers' first entry in 1970–71.

When Bill Fitch was named the first head coach, he said, "Just remember, the name is Fitch, not Houdini!" The Cavs lost their first 15 games before finally winning against fellow expansionist Portland. They lost 12 more in a row before they finally won a home game, this time against Buffalo, the third expansion team. And they were 2–34 at one point, before finishing 15–67. How bad did it get? One night Cavs' guard John Warren scored two points for Portland by making a lay-up in the wrong basket. Things weren't going too well for Portland, either. Its center, Leroy Ellis, tried to block the shot, and moments later, Portland tried to outdo the Cavs by playing six men.

Season Two was a bit better. The Cavs drafted Notre Dame guard Austin Carr and he averaged more than 20 points per game in each of the next three seasons. The Cavs improved to 23 wins, then 32, but slid in 1973–74 to 29–53. That off-season, the Cavs were able to acquire Jim Chones, Dick Snyder, Campy Russell and Foots Walker which became the nucleus for the next few years.

The Cavs went 40–42 in 1974–75, then qualified for their first playoffs by rolling to a 49–33 mark and the Central Division title in 1975–76. Their first-round opponent was Washington, which the Cavs disposed of in seven games. Snyder hit a running five-foot bank shot for the winner in Game 7 to send the Cavs into the Eastern Conference finals against the Boston Celtics. Chones broke a bone in a foot prior to the series and the Cavs ran out of players and gas, losing to the Celtics, 4–2. The Cavs suffered through more injuries the following year and fell to 43–39 and were eliminated in the first round of the playoffs by the Bullets, 3–1. It was more of the same in 1977–78. Same record. Same first-round playoff loss, this time to the New York Knicks, 2–0.

Faces changed as the Cavs limped through seasons of 30 and 37 wins before original owner Nick Mileti sold the team to Ted Stepien prior to the 1980–81 campaign. Stepien's first move was to hire Bill Musselman as head coach, and then he began making trades. Before he was through, he traded three No. 1 draft picks to the Dallas Mavericks in exchange for Mike Bratz, Richard Washington and Jerome Whitehead. By mid-season, he traded another No. 1 pick to Dallas, this time for Geoff Huston. The Cavs finished with a record of 28–54 and down four first-round picks. The revolving door continued the following season. Don Delaney opened the season as head coach, but was replaced by Chuck Daly on Dec. 4, 1981. Trade after trade was made. By the end of the season a total of 23 players had appeared in a Cavs uniform. The team lost its last 19 games and finished 15–67.

The 1982–83 season was marked by more player trades and a coaching change that ultimately resulted in a 23–59 record. But more importantly, it marked the end of the Stepien "Blue Light Specials." He sold the team to the Gund brothers. The NBA recognized the damage that Stepien had done to the franchise and awarded the Cavs four bonus first-round draft choices over the next four years.

The Cavs slowly returned to respectability. They revamped the line-up and won 28 games, then 36, 29, 31 and 42. They entered the 1988–89 season with high expectations. Lenny Wilkens was comfortably in place as the head coach. Young players Brad Daugherty, Mark Price and Ron Harper had gained experience, while veterans filled most of the back-up spots. The Cavs jumped out of the blocks at 7–1, then 11–3, and 24–5. At that point they had the best record in the NBA. They played solidly the rest of the way and finished the season with a 57–25 mark, including a 37–4 record at home in the Richfield Coliseum. The Cavs were already expecting a Conference finals match-up with the Detroit Pistons when they faced the Chicago Bulls in the first round of the playoffs. Someone forgot to tell Michael Jordan and the Bulls. Jordan hit a 16-foot jumper at the buzzer in Game 5 as the Bulls upset the Cavs, 3–2. The next year, the Cavs were forced to win their final six games to qualify for the playoffs, ending at 42–40. They were eliminated by Philadelphia in the playoffs, 3–2. Injuries plagued the Cavs the following season. They fell to 33–49 and out of the playoffs.

In 1991–92, the Cavs were healthy again and rebounded to a 57–25 record. They sailed past the New Jersey Nets in the first round of the playoffs, 3–1, and beat Boston, 4–3, to set up the Conference finals against Chicago. The Bulls and Jordan again proved they were too strong, winning the series 4–2.

The Cavs went 54–28 in 1992–93 behind Daugherty, Price and Larry Nance. The only problem was they again met the Bulls and Jordan in the playoffs. This time it was the second round and Chicago won, 4–0. Wilkens was forced out, because he couldn't take the club past the Bulls. Mike Fratello was named as his replacement prior to the 1993–94 season.

The Cavaliers fell to 47–35 and were swept in the first round of the playoffs by—you guessed it—the Bulls. In 1994–95, Daugherty was forced to sit out the entire season with a back injury and Price missed nearly half the year because of an assortment of ailments. The Cavs, who missed 267 man-games to injury/illness, limped home with a 43–39 record in the new Gund Arena and qualified for the playoffs. Fortunately they avoided the Bulls, but lost to the Knicks, 3 games to 1.

With Daugherty out again with injuries and Price dealt to Washington, Cleveland's expectations were low for the 1995–96 season. But the Cavs led the league in fewest points allowed (88.5 per game) for the second year in a row and improved to 47–35. They gained the home court advantage in the first round of the playoffs, but were upset by the Knicks, 3–0.

The Cavs again yielded the fewest points in 1996–97 and finished above .500 (42–40), but failed to make the playoffs. During the off-season the Cavs cleaned house. They brought in Shawn Kemp from Seattle in a three-team deal, then started three rookies. The result? A 47–35 record and a return to the playoffs.

In his first season in Cleveland, Shawn Kemp led the Cavs in points and rebounds.

INDIVIDUAL RECORDS

Career

    Points: 10,389, Brad Daugherty, 1986–94

    Rebounds: 5,227, Brad Daugherty, 1986–94

    Assists: 4,206, Mark Price, 1986–95

    Field Goal Pct.: .553, Mark West, 1984–88, 1996–97

    Free Throw Pct.: .906, Mark Price, 1986–95

Season

    Points: 2,012, Mike Mitchell, 1980–81

    Rebounds: 891, Jim Brewer, 1975–76

    Assists: 735, John Bagley, 1985–86

    Field Goal Pct.: .600, Tyrone Hill, 1996–97

    Free Throw Pct.: .948, Mark Price, 1992–93

ACROSS

1. Pass leading to a basket (abbr.)
3. Son of former Washington Bullets GM
6. Against (abbr.)
8. 2 quarters
10. Arizona guard acquired from Phoenix in '89 for 2nd round draft pick
11. Former
12. John Amaechi's alma mater (init.)
14. Team meal vegetable
15. Bring in the team meal
16. Furry creature Whammer
17. Before defeated or sportsmanlike
18. Washington St. guard signed as a free agent in '87
19. Schedules
20. ___ vs. Them
21. Weekend late-night TV show (init.)
23. 1st word of the national anthem
25. Places on the floor
28. Bobby Smith's nickname, et al.
30. Directs
32. Cavs' career assists leader
34. Bucks' Connecticut guard
36. Changes direction sharply
37. Cavs' career scoring leader
41. Blackman's nickname

42. Stretch
43. The ReignMan
45. Back-up players
47. Go ___ guy
48. Make defensive stand
50. Oregon guard was Cavs' 1st round pick in '91
52. Carom at own basket (init.)
53. Away
54. NBA's cable TV network
55. Minor league (init.)
57. John Johnson's alma mater (init.)
58. Arena music makers
59. Omit
60. Luxury boxes for fans
61. World B.

DOWN

2. Teams
3. Cavs' head coach
4. Where severely injured players are sent (init.)
5. Season
7. Whirlpool
8. Ref ___ Hollins
9. Corporation granted by NBA
10. Boots
13. 3.4 apg, .533 or 21.3 ppg

14. Tugs
15. Refs' decisions
20. ___ and in
22. A cheer
24. Hot Rod
26. Qtr.
27. Cavs' division
29. Cavs' owners
31. Swat
33. Notre Dame's Austin or N.C. St.'s Kenny
35. Media guide head shots
38. Made 15 consecutive shots vs. Lakers in '84
39. Throw the ball away (abbr.)
40. Bottom half of a uniform
42. After locker or training
43. East coast rival
44. Tallies (abbr.)
46. Usual college class of drafted players (abbr.)
47. Football stat (abbr.)
49. Lane
51. Set Cavs record with 243 blocked shots in '92
52. Ahead: ___ top
54. Series of road games
56. Arena signs

Solution on page 178

RETIRED UNIFORM NUMBERS

7	Bingo Smith	42	Nate Thurmond
22	Larry Nance	43	Brad Daugherty
34	Austin Carr		

```
O  H  S  R  J  K  D  N  O  M  R  U  H  T  B
F  R  A  T  E  L  L  O  I  E  H  R  B  T  A
O  W  T  H  G  I  N  K  L  R  C  L  R  I  G
G  I  I  R  B  O  E  I  G  R  T  J  A  M  L
S  L  L  U  A  S  M  W  A  N  I  W  N  S  E
N  K  L  S  G  L  E  A  U  A  F  E  D  R  Y
L  E  I  S  L  S  H  E  S  O  R  K  O  R  L
L  N  W  E  T  T  C  F  K  R  E  N  O  L  L
E  S  H  L  H  N  M  H  A  D  E  P  L  I  F
H  I  L  L  A  L  E  C  S  U  R  L  D  E  R
C  I  R  N  D  H  O  S  R  I  E  A  R  H  E
T  J  O  H  N  S  O  N  C  T  N  R  E  C  W
I  O  E  O  A  U  B  E  A  G  Y  A  T  B  E
M  H  T  I  M  S  S  M  A  I  L  L  I  W  R
T  D  A  U  G  H  E  R  T  Y  N  D  O  B  B
```

BAGLEY	FITCH	NANCE
BEARD	FRATELLO	PRICE
BRANDON	FREE	RUSSELL
BREWER	HILL	SMITH
CARR	ILGAUSKAS	THURMOND
DAUGHERTY	JOHNSON	WEST
EHLO	KNIGHT	WILKENS
FERRY	MITCHELL	WILLIAMS

DALLAS MAVERICKS

The model franchise. Both on the court and off. If any team in the NBA wanted success, just follow the blueprint of the Dallas Mavericks. But somewhere along the way, the model franchise hit a wall. A brick wall. A very big, thick brick wall.

The Mavericks went from nearly winning the Western Conference finals against the Los Angeles Lakers in 1987–88 to one of the worst teams in the history of professional basketball in 1992–93. There are a lot of people, including those in the front office of the Mavericks, who are trying to figure out just what went wrong. There are no sure answers, yet.

The city of Dallas was awarded an expansion franchise Apr. 28, 1980. UCLA's Kiki Vandeweghe was the first player selected by the Mavericks in the college draft (11th overall pick). Dick Motta was named the head coach and Bob Weiss his assistant. Among the veteran players obtained through the dispersal draft were Jim Spanarkel, Tom LaGarde, Abdul Jeelani and Marty Byrnes. General Manager Norm Sonju wasted little time in dealing players and draft picks. He found an easy mark in Cleveland's owner, Ted Stepien. He soon had four future first-round picks from the Cavaliers and two others from the Denver Nuggets. A decision was made to build slowly through the draft.

The Mavericks won only 15 games in that first season. They showed improvement in one form or another in each of the next seven years. Over that period they drafted: Mark Aguirre (1981), Rolando Blackman (1981), Jay Vincent (1981), Dale Ellis (1983), Derek Harper (1983), Sam Perkins (1984), Detlef Schrempf (1985) and Roy Tarpley (1986).

Their victory total went from 15 to 28 to 38 to 43 to 44 to 44 (with a first-round playoff win) to 55 to 53 (with an appearance in the Conference finals). Motta was the coach through 1986–87. John MacLeod became the coach for the 1987–88 season in the Conference finals. He lasted only a year and half longer. What transpired then is anybody's guess.

The players drafted in the first round from 1988–91 were:

1988—No one (traded to Miami in the expansion draft)

1989—Randy White (8th overall pick)

1990—No one (traded to Sacramento for Rodney McCray)

1991—Doug Smith (6th overall pick)

Also during that period the Mavericks made these trades:

1989—Traded Mark Aguirre to Detroit for Adrian Dantley

1989—Traded Detlef Schrempf and a second-round draft pick to Indiana for Herb Williams

1990—Traded two first-round draft picks to Denver for Fat Lever

1990—Traded two first-round draft picks and Bill Wennington to Sacramento for Rodney McCray and two second-round picks

1992—Traded James Donaldson to New York for Brian Quinnett

1992—Traded Blackman to New York for a first-round pick

1992—Traded McCray to Chicago for a first-round pick and two second-round selections

In the midst of all that, Tarpley was banned from the league for repeated drug use, MacLeod departed and was replaced by Richie Adubato who was replaced by Gar Heard.

The Conference finals were followed the next season by a 38–44 mark. That improved to 47–35. But then the bottom dropped out. The Mavericks won just 28 games in 1990–91 and 22 in 1991–92. The fans in Dallas would just as soon forget about the 1992–93 season entirely.

The Mavericks flirted with the all-time NBA record for futility by going 11–71. They didn't win their 10th and 11th games until the final month. Nine wins by the 1972–73 Philadelphia 76ers remain the record. How bad was it? For trivia buffs years from now, here are the cold facts: The Mavericks lost 58 of their games by 10 or more points and the average margin of defeat was 15.2 points a game. They were last in the league in shooting percentage (.435) and last in opponents' shooting percentage (.501).

The Mavericks were able to sign first-round draft pick Jim Jackson 54 games into that season. They added Jamal Mashburn in the 1993 draft and named Quinn Buckner the head coach. So, what was the result for 1993–94? An improvement to 13 wins. The Mavs lost more games than any team in the league, by an average of 8.7 points per outing. They were 1–23 at one point and had losing streaks of 16, 17 and 20 games. They won five of their final 11 games to avoid finishing worse than the previous year.

Buckner was released and replaced by Motta. And Jason Kidd was selected in the 1994 draft. Dallas catapulted to 36 wins and the franchise seemed on the road to recovery.

But in 1995–96 Mashburn missed all but 18 games due to injuries and Kidd and Jackson had an on going feud. That spelled doom and the Mavericks fell to 26–56. It prompted Donald Carter, the franchise's original owner, to sell the team to a group of investors led by Ross Perot, Jr. Jim Cleamons, a member of the 1972 NBA champion L.A. Lakers and an assistant coach with the Chicago Bulls' four title teams, was named the new head coach, while long-time president Norm Sonju stepped down.

The changes didn't help much. The Mavericks were 24–58 in Cleamons' first season. He was replaced on the bench in the middle of the 1997–98 season by G.M. Don Nelson. Dallas finished 20–62. The Mavericks used the sixth pick in the 1998 draft to select Michigan's Robert Traylor, then immediately traded him to Milwaukee for draftees Dirk Nowitzki and Pat Garrity. Before the night was over, Garrity, too, was traded, along with Martin Muursepp, Bubba Wells and a future draft choice to Phoenix for guard Steve Nash.

Copyright © 1997 Brian Spurlock/Spurlock Photography, Inc.

Michael Finely was named to the NBA's All-Rookie first team in 1996.

INDIVIDUAL RECORDS

Career

    Points: 16,643, Rolando Blackman, 1981–92

    Rebounds: 4,589, James Donaldson, 1985–92

    Assists: 5,111, Derek Harper, 1983–94, 1996–97

    Field Goal Pct.: .551, James Donaldson, 1985–92

    Free Throw Pct.: .857, Jim Spanarkel, 1980–84

Season

    Points: 2,330, Mark Aguirre, 1983–84

    Rebounds: 973, James Donaldson, 1986–87

    Assists: 783, Jason Kidd, 1995–96

    Field Goal Pct.: .586, James Donaldson, 1986–87

    Free Throw Pct.: .898, Rolando Blackman, 1991–92

ACROSS

2. Swap
8. 1-pointer (init.)
10. The ball is full of it
11. Mavericks' career scoring leader
14. Precipitation
16. Stomach muscle (abbr.)
18. Ricochets
19. Vends
20. A division
22. 1st word of the national anthem
24. Carom at own basket (init.)
25. Sound of crowd displeasure
27. ___ or die
29. Primary
30. Mark Aguirre's alma mater (init.)
31. Cowboys' rival league (init.)
32. Popeye
33. Column heading on box score (init.)
35. Away
37. North Carolina forward was Mavericks' 1st round pick in '84
39. Play-___-play announcer
40. Cheer in unison
42. ___-captain
43. Set Mavericks record with 2,330 points in 1983–84
47. Players get 6 per game (init.)

48. Locker room aroma
49. Make a basket
51. Before fake or after double
53. Extra period (abbr.)
54. All right
55. ___ shoots, he scores!
56. Type of x ray (init.)
58. Sam and Jay
59. Roster spot for hurt players (init.)
60. Exercise for the triceps
61. Column heading on roster (abbr.)
63. Cherokee Parks' alma mater (init.)
64. Dunk
67. Defunct rival league (init.)
70. '88 Western Conference finals foe (init.)
71. Basket cord
73. Ref's relative
74. Dribble hard to the basket
75. Trick defense: ___-and-1

DOWN

1. Players' rep on the floor
2. Appearance before a judge
3. Selection of college players
4. Column heading on standings (init.)
5. Mavericks' leading scorer in 1993–94 and 1995–96
6. Jamal Mashburn's alma mater (init.)
7. ___-announcer (init.)
9. Taps
12. Mavericks' leading scorer in 1994–95
13. Don and Donn
15. NBA's TV network
17. Halftime twirler's tool
21. Uwe Blab's alma mater (init.)
23. Mavericks' career assists leader
26. Postseason
27. Mavericks' career rebounding leader
28. Dream Team: Team ___
29. Team physician (init.)
34. Kareem's ___ Hook
36. Dennis Nutt's alma mater (init.)
38. Detlef
41. Dismissed from NBA for violation of drug policy
44. Small devil
45. 1st year player
46. Slate of games
50. Has played more games than any Maverick
52. Mavericks' head coach, twice
57. Up and ___
62. In and ___
65. Clarence Kea's alma mater (init.)
66. Jerome Whitehead's alma mater (init.)
68. Arena sign
69. Derek Harper's alma mater (init.)
71. On the back of a jersey (abbr.)
72. Former

Solution on page 178

RETIRED UNIFORM NUMBERS

15   Brad Davis

```
T  S  C  H  R  E  M  P  F  O  M  V  T  N  D
U  P  N  A  S  N  I  K  R  E  P  A  S  O  O
D  A  N  T  L  E  Y  M  O  A  R  N  O  S  N
A  N  T  N  E  C  N  I  V  P  O  D  G  L  A
N  A  O  R  L  E  R  M  L  M  D  E  F  E  L
N  R  Z  D  D  O  E  A  I  L  W  I  N  D
I  K  K  E  N  T  Y  E  K  L  A  E  N  E  S
M  E  I  M  T  E  L  L  I  C  H  G  L  D  O
P  L  D  A  N  C  E  S  K  I  R  H  E  O  N
H  J  D  N  Y  Y  I  R  L  A  K  E  Y  E  U
A  J  A  C  K  S  O  N  G  P  C  A  S  L  S
R  S  I  V  A  D  Y  E  L  D  A  R  B  C  T
P  N  I  K  R  E  P  N  R  U  B  H  S  A  M
E  A  G  U  I  R  R  E  Y  A  R  C  C  M  N
R  Y  B  L  A  C  K  M  A  N  E  N  E  W  P
```

AGUIRRE	FINLEY	MOTTA
BLACKMAN	GREEN	NELSON
BRADLEY	HARPER	PERKINS
CLEAMONS	JACKSON	SCHREMPF
DANTLEY	KIDD	SPANARKAL
DAVIS	MACLEOD	TARPLEY
DONALDSON	MASHBURN	VANDEWEGHE
ELLIS	MCCRAY	VINCENT

DENVER NUGGETS

The Denver Nuggets began as the Denver "Ringsby Rockets," one of the 11 original franchises in the American Basketball Association in 1967–68.

The original Rockets were owned by trucking executive Bill Ringsby and sons. Bob Bass was the first coach, and he led the club to 45- and 44-win seasons in the first two years. In the summer of 1969, the Rockets signed U.S. Olympic team hero Spencer Haywood, a college undergraduate. John McClendon was named head coach, but was replaced 28 games into the season by Joe Belmont. Under Belmont, the Rockets won 42 of their final 56 games to finish 51–33. That was good enough to win the Western Division, but the Rockets were eliminated in the second round of the playoffs. Haywood averaged 29.9 points and 19.5 rebounds a game and was named the league's Most Valuable Player and Rookie of the Year.

Haywood left the Rockets prior to the 1970–71 season (he eventually signed with Seattle in the NBA). Belmont was fired after the club started 3–10, and he was replaced by assistant Stan Albeck. The Rockets wound up 30–54 and were eliminated in a one-game playoff.

Following that season, Ringsby lured Alex Hannum, coach of the San Diego Rockets in the NBA, to Denver to be president, general manager and head coach. In his first season, the Rockets were 34–50, and qualified for the playoffs. In 1972–73, the Rockets improved to 47–37, but injuries to three of their starters in the playoffs cost them a shot at the ABA title. It was in the midst of that season that the franchise was sold to a group of San Diego businessmen headed by Frank Goldberg and Bud Fischer.

They watched their club slump to 37–47 in 1973–74 and decided that changes were in order. First, they hired Carl Scheer as president and general manager. He quickly named Larry Brown the new head coach. Then they changed the team's logo, colors and nickname to "Nuggets."

All of the changes paid off. The Nuggets went 65–19 and won the Western Division championship, but were eliminated by the Indiana Pacers in the Division finals. The Nuggets followed that with another Division title, going 60–24, and made it to the ABA championship series before being eliminated by the New York Nets.

The ABA had been on shaky financial ground for the entire season and was forced to cease operations in the summer of 1976. The Nuggets, though, were one of four ABA teams merged into the NBA. Despite the new competition, the Nuggets didn't miss a beat. Led by David Thompson, Dan Issel and Bobby

Jones, Denver won the Midwest Division with a 50–32 record. The Nuggets were eliminated in the first round of the playoffs and returned the following season hungrier than ever. They again won the Midwest Division, even though their record slid to 48–34. They advanced to the Western Conference finals before losing to the Seattle SuperSonics, 4 games to 2. The 1978–79 season saw another decline. Brown stepped down as coach after a 28–25 start and was replaced by Donnie Walsh. The Nuggets finished strong under Walsh and qualified for the playoffs, but were eliminated in the first round.

The Nuggets missed the playoffs in each of the next two seasons and Walsh was replaced by Doug Moe midway through the 1980–81 campaign. Moe remained in that capacity for the next nine-and-a-half years. The Nuggets and their fans took a liking to Moe immediately. Denver returned to prominence in the West, finishing first or second in their division four times. In all, Moe won 432 games (an average of 45 victories a year), but never made it into the NBA Finals.

After Moe left following the 1989–90 season, the Nuggets entered their most exciting, but least successful, period. Enter Head Coach Paul Westhead. He arrived from Loyola Marymount where one of his teams averaged 122.4 points in each 40-minute game, including 186 in one contest.

The Nuggets would run and gun and soon became known as "Enver" (as in no "D"). Opposing teams envisioned 200-point games. It didn't quite come to that, but the Nuggets did give up 173, 162 and 161. And that was just in the first week of the season. Westhead revised his attack after the club got off to a 6–28 start. It rallied, somewhat, and finished the season at 20–62, the worst record in Denver's history. That team led the NBA in scoring with 119.9 points per game, but it also set an NBA record by giving up 130.8 points per outing.

In 1991–92 the Nuggets improved to 24–58, but it marked the end of Westhead's career and the end of the pinball-like scoreboard. Issel was named as the 10th Nuggets' head coach in the summer of 1992 and led them back to respectability with a 36–46 mark. The Nuggets improved to 42–40 in 1993–94 and advanced in the playoffs for the first time in six years. The Nuggets, the eighth and final seed in the Western Conference, pulled off the biggest upset in the history of the NBA playoffs. They beat Seattle, which had the best record in the league and the No. 1 seed, 3 games to 2. Denver then stretched Utah to seven games before bowing out in the second round.

But Issel departed midway through the 1994–95 season, and he was replaced, first by Gene Littles, then Bernie Bickerstaff. The Nuggets wound up 41–41 and were eliminated in the first round of the playoffs.

In 1995–96, Denver was led by center Dikembe Mutombo, who was tops in the NBA in blocked shots (4.5 per game) and third in the league in rebounds (11.8 per game). The Nuggets fell to 35–47, though, when the team was embroiled in controversy for much of the year over Mahmoud Abdul-Rauf's refusal to stand for the national anthem. At the end of the season, Abdul-Rauf was dealt to Sacramento and Mutombo left after becoming a free agent.

The Nuggets fell to 21–61 in 1996–97; Bickerstaff was replaced early in the year by Dick Motta. The following season Bill Hanzlik was hired as head coach, but the Nuggets barely avoided the worst record in NBA history at 11–71. Gone was Hanzlik and basketball V.P. Allan Bristow. Returning to the front office was Issel.

LaPhonso Ellis was a first-round pick of the Nuggets in the 1992 draft.

INDIVIDUAL RECORDS
Career

    Points: 21,645, Alex English, 1979–90

    Rebounds: 6,630, Dan Issel, 1975–85

    Assists: 3,679, Alex English, 1979–90

    Field Goal Pct.: .573, Bobby Jones, 1976–78

    Free Throw Pct.: .916, Mahmoud Abdul-Rauf, 1990–96

Season

    Points: 2,414, Alex English, 1985–86

    Rebounds: 1,070, Dikembe Mutombo, 1992–93

    Assists: 693, Michael Adams, 1990–91

    Field Goal Pct.: .580, Kiki Vandeweghe, 1983–84

    Free Throw Pct.: .956, Mahmoud Abdul-Rauf, 1993–94

ACROSS

2. Provided uniforms for Zaire women's basketball team at '96 Olympics
9. Capable
11. Player getting position under the boards
13. Nuggets' career field goal pct. leader
14. ___ vs. Them
18. Column heading on standings (init.)
19. Top of the ___
20. Rested on the bench
22. Regulation
23. ___ shoots, he scores!
24. Nuggets' career rebounding leader
25. Deadlock
27. Wayne Rollins' nickname
30. Kiki and Ernie
33. Former
34. New York's time zone (init.)
35. Credit card of choice at box office
37. ___ and out
38. Equipment tote
40. Swats
42. Breakfast drink (init.)
44. Throw the ball away (abbr.)
45. Fat

46. Tip
48. Big George
50. Referee's tool
52. Height of rim in feet
53. 4.5 rpg, 4-of-6, 45 asts. (abbr.)
56. Courts
58. Alley-oop pass
59. Fastbreaking
63. Type of shot
64. Lines
65. Arm joint

DOWN

1. ___-announcer (init.)
2. Play ___ or trade me!
3. Scored 73 points in '78 game
4. Come upon
5. Carom at own basket (init.)
6. Shoot a lot
7. Arena signs
8. Bounce the ball
10. Rim
12. Huge
15. Play-___-play announcer
16. Brian Williams' alma mater (init.)
17. Vending machine coin opening
20. Not fast

21. Rugged
22. Michigan guard was Nuggets' 1st round pick in '94
26. Tied
28. Baseball stat (init.)
29. Star of the game
31. Away
32. Nuggets' career scoring leader
35. Against (abbr.)
36. Eat up the clock
38. Word in bio before 4-10-66
39. One of the items in a program of sports
40. Nuggets' coach, 1974–79
41. Feel a sudden rush
43. Led the NBA in assists in 1996–97
47. Marcus Liberty's alma mater (init.)
49. NE Louisiana forward was an '85 all-star
51. Blows 50 Across
54. Double team
55. Finishes
56. 2-pointer (init.)
57. ___ pick (2 words)
60. Treat a sprained ankle
61. Extra period (abbr.)
62. A cheer

Solution on page 179

RETIRED UNIFORM NUMBERS

2	Alex English
33	David Thompson
40	Byron Beck
44	Dan Issel

```
U  J  I  J  L  S  C  N  N  I  V  L  A  C  E
Y  A  Y  E  O  F  C  U  N  N  M  L  I  O  H
B  C  R  X  J  N  V  O  D  U  N  O  L  O  I
A  K  E  C  K  A  E  S  T  S  N  I  E  P  M
D  S  C  J  O  E  B  S  N  T  S  D  X  E  L
I  O  E  E  A  B  A  A  I  C  U  P  L  R  T
F  N  A  L  B  U  V  S  L  N  O  E  V  I  H
U  H  C  D  L  E  S  O  N  I  V  E  S  N  O
O  A  Y  T  A  I  B  S  T  E  R  S  E  O  M
B  N  L  N  V  M  S  R  R  T  E  A  Y  S  P
M  Z  E  A  O  E  S  I  O  L  T  L  E  P  S
O  L  D  N  K  N  O  S  P  W  I  A  M  M  O
T  I  M  C  G  I  N  N  I  S  N  H  N  I  N
U  K  I  H  J  O  N  M  C  D  Y  E  S  S  I
M  B  E  N  G  L  I  S  H  G  H  E  T  K  W
```

ADAMS	ENGLISH	MCDYESS
BECK	EVANS	MCGINNIS
BROWN	HANZLIK	MOE
CALVIN	ISSEL	MUTOMBO
COOPER	JABALI	NATT
DAVIS	JACKSON	SCOTT
DUNN	JONES	SIMPSON
ELLIS	LEVER	THOMPSON

DETROIT PISTONS

They were the Ft. Wayne Pistons and the Detroit Pistons. And then they were Chuck Daly's Pistons.

It's easy to make the separations. In nine years at Ft. Wayne, the Pistons won three playoff series and went 17–27 in post-season play. In the first 26 seasons in Detroit, the Pistons won three playoff series and went 23–34 in post-season play. They failed to qualify for the playoffs in 15 of those years.

As for Daly's Pistons? He was the head coach nine years. They never won less than 46 games in a season and qualified for the playoffs every year. They won 16 playoff series and went 71–42 in post-season play with two NBA championships. Daly left the Pistons following the 1991–92 season. So what happened then? They failed to make the playoffs for three straight years and dropped to just 20 wins in an entire season.

Ft. Wayne entered the NBA in 1948–49 with Carl Bennett the head coach. When the Pistons failed to win in their first six contests, he was replaced by Paul Armstrong, and they ended the year at 22–38. The Pistons' stay in Ft. Wayne was uneventful, except for 1954–55. The Pistons won the Western Division with a 43–29 record and received a bye in the first round of the playoffs. They defeated the three-time defending champion Minneapolis Lakers in the Western Division finals, 3 games to 1. That set up a championship series against the Syracuse Nationals. The Pistons lost the first two games in Syracuse and returned home to find their home arena already booked for another event. No one had expected the Pistons to get that far. So they played their "home" games in Indianapolis. The Pistons won all three games in Indiana and sent the series back to Syracuse. The Nationals won Game 6, 109–104, then nipped the Pistons in Game 7, 92–91.

The Pistons moved to Detroit prior to the 1957–58 season. Even with bona fide all-stars George Yardley, Gene Shue, Dick McGuire, Walter Dukes, Chuck Noble, Bailey Howell, Terry Dischinger, Dave DeBusschere and Eddie Miles, the Pistons were stuck in idle near the bottom of the pack. The Pistons went through 15 consecutive losing seasons before going 45–37 in 1970–71. The trio of Dave Bing, Jimmy Walker and Bob Lanier revived the Pistons and brought them respectability through most of the 1970s. The Pistons hit a lull in 1978–79 (30–52) and 1979–80 (16–66) under coaches Dick Vitale and Richie Adubato.

General Manager Jack McCloskey was hired midway through that 1979–80 season. From that point on, he began sculpting a championship team. In 1981–

82 he added Isiah Thomas through the draft and Bill Laimbeer and Vinnie Johnson through trades. In 1983–84 he added Daly as the head coach. In 1985–86 he added Rick Mahorn through a trade and Joe Dumars through the draft. In 1986–87 he added John Salley and Dennis Rodman through the draft. In 1987–88 he added James Edwards through a trade and then completed the key roster spots midway through the 1988–89 season by adding Mark Aguirre through a trade.

That group began to gel immediately. The Pistons won 49 games in 1983–84, followed by 46 and 46. Then came 1986–87—the Pistons had their best season ever at 52–30. They entered the playoffs and beat the Washington Bullets, 3–1. They breezed past the Atlanta Hawks in the second round, 4–1, and reached the Eastern Conference finals against the Boston Celtics. The Pistons lost, 4–3.

The following season the Pistons had their sights set on improvement. The only way to improve on the previous season was to get to the championship series and that they did. They went 54–28 in the regular season, then beat Washington and the Chicago Bulls in the first two rounds of the playoffs. That set up a rematch with the Celtics. This time the Pistons won, 4–2. But Detroit lost in the Finals, 4–3, to the Los Angeles Lakers.

In 1988–89, the Pistons again had their sights set on improvement. The only way to improve on the previous season was to win the championship. And they did. They went 63–19 during the regular season, then beat Boston, Milwaukee and Chicago to set up a rematch with the Lakers in the championship series. This time the Pistons won, 4–0. They went through the playoffs with a 15–2 record on their way to the franchise's first title.

What was left for improvement? How about winning two championships in a row? They did that, too. They went 59–23 in the regular season, then beat Indiana, New York and Chicago to set up a championship series with the Portland Trail Blazers. Detroit wouldn't be denied its second title and won the series, 4–1.

The Pistons were unable to "three-peat" in 1990–91, losing to Chicago in the Conference finals, but still won 50 games. They won 48 in 1991–92. By then age, trades and expansion had begun to pull the team apart. Daly decided he was ready for new challenges and he, too, departed.

The Pistons slipped to 40–42 in 1992–93 under Ron Rothstein. Then came massive changes. Don Chaney replaced Rothstein; Rodman was traded; Laimbeer retired a month into the season; and Thomas called it quits at the end of a the long 20–62 season.

Led by rookie Grant Hill, the Pistons improved slightly to 28–54 in 1994–95, but Chaney was replaced by Doug Collins. He sparked the Pistons to a 46–36 record and their first playoff appearance in the post-Daly era. Hill averaged 20.2 points per game, Allan Houston 19.7 and Otis Thorpe 14.2.

The Pistons improved to 54–28 in 1996–97, but were beaten in the first round of the playoffs by Atlanta, 3 games to 2. In 1997–98, the Pistons got off to a slow start and patience disappeared. Tempers flared. Collins was replaced on the sidelines by Alvin Gentry and the Pistons closed to a 37–45 mark and out of the playoffs.

Grant Hill has played in the All-Star Game in each of his four NBA seasons.

INDIVIDUAL RECORDS

Career

    Points: 18,822, Isiah Thomas, 1981–94

    Rebounds: 9,430, Bill Laimbeer, 1981–94

    Assists: 9,061, Isiah Thomas, 1981–94

    Field Goal Pct.: .537, Dennis Rodman, 1986–93

    Free Throw Pct.: .851, Bill Laimbeer, 1981–94

Season

    Points: 2,213, Dave Bing, 1970–71

    Rebounds: 1,530, Dennis Rodman, 1991–92

    Assists: 1,123, Isiah Thomas, 1984–85

    Field Goal Pct.: .595, Dennis Rodman, 1988–89

    Free Throw Pct.: .900, Joe Dumars, 1989–90

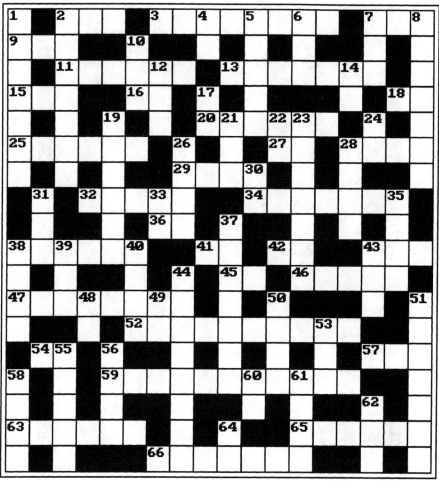

ACROSS

2. Trot
3. Happy
7. NBA's TV network
9. Capacity crowd (init.)
11. Averaged 21.1 ppg from 1959–64
13. Pistons' division
15. Hotel
16. Throw the ball away (abbr.)
18. 1-pointer (init.)
20. The ___ of Auburn Hills
25. Pistons' career scoring leader
27. Go ___ guy
28. Joe Dumars' uniform number
29. Eliminate
32. ___ Smith
34. Arkansas center Oliver and family
36. Extra period (abbr.)
38. A captain of Dream Team II at '94 World Championships
41. Home to the Wizards (init.)
42. Up and ___
43. ___ Shammgod
45. Carom at own basket (init.)
46. Attempt to score
47. Pistons' career rebounding leader
52. Vitale-ism for big-game player
54. Before Adoo, Elroy or Queen

57. Carom (abbr.)
59. U. of Detroit forward also pitched in the big leagues
63. Basket
65. Pick
66. Notre Dame forward was Pistons' leading scorer in 1986–87 and 1987–88

DOWN

1. Passes leading to baskets
2. Lee, Ron or Vinnie
4. Roster spot for hurt players (init.)
5. Take the ball away
6. Before of bounds or after fouled
7. Lions' rival league (init.)
8. Pivot men
10. Wager on a game
12. Alley-oop pass
14. Arena sign
17. Wire service (init.)
19. Traded in 1980 to Milwaukee after averaging 22.7 ppg in 10 years
21. Stomach muscles (abbr.)
22. Away
23. Pistons head coach released in '98

24. ___ or die
26. 6-___-10
28. Part of FTA
30. Logo registration (abbr.)
31. Malik Sealy's alma mater (init.)
33. A cheer
35. Jump, hook or set
37. Players who make baskets
38. Pistons' championship head coach
39. Type of x ray (init.)
40. Trod
43. He ___ Game
44. Set Pistons record with 56 points in '83 game
48. Don Kojis' alma mater (init.)
49. Where severely injured players are sent (init.)
50. Reggie Harding's last level of education: ___ School
51. Grab a missed shot
53. Hearing organ
55. Mentor
56. At rest
58. Back-up players
60. ___-captain
61. Lay-up: ___ shot
62. Basket cord
64. Kept on the scoreboard (abbr.)

Solution on page 179

RETIRED UNIFORM NUMBERS

2	Chuck Daly	16	Bob Lanier
11	Isiah Thomas	21	Dave Bing
15	Vinnie Johnson	40	Bill Laimbeer

```
B   W   J   S   G   U   I   S   N   I   L   L   O   C   D
R   R   O   V   I   T   A   L   E   O   Y   D   E   N   A
R   Y   H   R   A   O   O   H   N   R   A   I   T   I   N
J   E   N   U   E   R   I   G   S   I   U   S   M   W   T
B   L   S   O   N   L   O   L   H   S   T   C   I   A   L
W   A   O   K   L   T   L   B   U   R   E   H   R   L   E
G   N   N   R   T   I   E   I   E   S   R   I   O   K   Y
Z   N   C   R   M   E   L   R   H   O   H   N   W   E   T
T   R   I   P   U   C   K   A   W   H   S   G   Y   R   B
H   L   U   B   O   D   W   E   S   L   S   E   E   N   R
O   D   I   C   U   E   T   S   N   L   L   R   L   S   O
M   R   R   M   L   R   U   S   R   A   M   U   L   O   W
A   D   A   L   Y   Y   A   R   D   L   E   Y   A   N   N
S   R   L   A   N   I   E   R   N   T   L   E   S   D   N
S   R   E   E   B   M   I   A   L   R   O   D   M   A   N
```

BING	HUNTER	ROWE
BROWN	JOHNSON	SALLEY
COLLINS	LAIMBEER	SHUE
DALY	LANIER	THOMAS
DANTLEY	LONG	TRIPUCKA
DISCHINGER	MILLS	VITALE
DUMARS	OHL	WALKER
HILL	RODMAN	YARDLEY

GOLDEN STATE WARRIORS

The Boston Celtics can brag about their 16 NBA titles. The Lakers can talk about their 11 championships. Even let the Chicago Bulls mention their three rings in a row. But none of them accomplished what the Warriors did and none ever will. You see, the Warriors won the very first NBA championship.

It was 1946–47 and the Warriors were then playing in Philadelphia. The Warriors went 35–25 and finished second in the Eastern Division by 14 games behind the Washington Capitols. But the Warriors caught on fire in the playoffs. They eliminated the St. Louis Bombers, 2 games to 1, in the first round. They defeated the New York Knickerbockers in the second round, 2–0, while the Capitols were losing to the Chicago Stags in the semifinals. That set up the first NBA Finals between Philadelphia and Chicago. The Warriors won, 4–1. That first team was coached by the legendary Eddie Gottlieb and included Joe Fulks (who led the league in scoring with 23.2 points a game), Angelo Musi and Matt Goukas.

The following season, the Warriors proved their championship was no fluke. In the regular season, they won the Eastern Division with a record of 27–21 and reached the Finals before losing to the Baltimore Bullets, 4–2. Gottlieb remained the coach through 1954–55, but the Warriors never were able to duplicate their early success. George Senesky was named head coach in 1955–56 and immediately turned around the Warriors' fortunes. Behind Paul Arizin (a nine-time all-star who averaged more than 20 points a game as a Warrior) and Neil Johnston (a three-time league scoring champ), Philadelphia went from last place in the standings in 1954–55 to the NBA title in 1955–56.

Not only did the Warriors make a good choice in the summer of 1955 to make Senesky their coach, but they also had the foresight to use their No. 1 pick in the draft to select local high school phenom Wilt Chamberlain as a territorial choice eligible in 1959. The wait was well worth it. The Warriors hovered around the .500 mark until Chamberlain arrived for the 1959–60 season. His rookie season was, statistically, the greatest ever. He averaged 37.6 points and 27.0 rebounds a game. The Warriors went from 32 wins to 49 wins.

Chamberlain continued to dominate the game. He scored 100 points against the Knicks, Mar. 2, 1962. He led the league in scoring each year (including an incredible 50.4 points a game in 1961–62) and was first or second in rebounds until the Warriors traded him Jan. 15, 1965. The Warriors moved from Philadelphia to San Francisco in the summer of 1962. Chamberlain yearned for home, and Philadelphia and the new 76ers yearned for Wilt. The Warriors received Connie Dierking, Paul Neumann, Lee Shaffer and an undisclosed amount of cash in exchange for Chamberlain.

The Warriors were a very good team with Chamberlain, but never reached the league championship series with him. With him gone, though, the Warriors plummeted. They went 17–63 in 1964–65, but used the fourth overall pick in the college draft to select Rick Barry, the NCAA scoring champion from Miami (Fla.). The sharp-shooter had an instant impact. He averaged 25.7 points a game as a rookie and helped the Warriors improve to 35–45.

Barry led the league in scoring in 1966–67 with 35.6 points a game. He helped lead the Warriors to a 44–37 record, first place in the Western Division and a berth in the NBA Finals. The Warriors lost to the Philadelphia 76ers in the Finals, 4–2. Everything was looking up again for the Warriors. But the American Basketball Association was formed in the summer of 1967 and attracted the attention of Barry who left the Warriors and the NBA. Barry was gone for five years before returning for the 1972–73 season.

During his absence, the Warriors moved across the bay from San Francisco to Oakland and became known as the Golden State Warriors in 1971–72. By then former Warrior great Al Attles was the head coach. The Warriors had a strong squad with Nate Thurmond, Jeff Mullins, Cazzie Russell and Jim Barnett. They won 51 games in 1971–72, then 47 and 44. In 1974–75, with Barry, Keith Wilkes, Butch Beard, Clifford Ray and Charles Johnson, the Warriors went 48–34 to win the Pacific Division. They beat the Seattle SuperSonics and the Chicago Bulls in the playoffs to set up a Finals match against the Washington Bullets. Golden State won the championship, 4–0.

They improved to 59 wins the following year, but lost in the Conference finals. The key players began to leave through free agency and trades and the Warriors went from 1978 to 1986 without qualifying for the playoffs. After a year at 42–40 under George Karl, they fell to 20 wins in 1987–88 and Don Nelson arrived in the summer of 1988 as the coach, general manager and part-owner. Nelson's teams yo-yoed from 55 wins in 1991–92 to 34 victories in 1992–93, back to 50 wins in 1993–94.

During the 1993 college draft, the Warriors identified Chris Webber as the big man that could plug their constant hole in the middle. Golden State gave up three future first-round picks and the draft rights to Anfernee Hardaway to get Webber. The 6-foot-10 Michigan Wolverine didn't disappoint anyone when he was named the NBA Rookie of the Year after averaging 17.5 points and 9.1 rebounds a game. But a feud between Nelson and Webber couldn't be resolved and Webber was shipped to the Washington Bullets on Nov. 17, 1994 in exchange for Tom Gugliotta and three future first-round draft picks.

Nelson—nor the team—ever recovered. Nellie quit halfway through the season and was replaced by Bob Lanier. The Warriors fell to 26–56, but drew the No. 1 overall selection in the college draft. They chose 6-foot-10 forward Joe Smith out of Maryland. Directed by new coach Rick Adelman, the Warriors went 36–46 in 1995–96 and missed the playoffs by three games. A 30–52 mark the following year caused Adelman to depart and P.J. Carlesimo was brought in from Portland to coach the team.

Carlesimo and all-star guard Latrell Sprewell did not get along. Sprewell attempted to choke Carlesimo, was suspended for the entire season and debates continued for the duration of the season on whether the penalty fit the crime. Hidden in the controversy was the Warriors' 19–63 record and empty arena in its premiere season.

Chris Mullin scored 16,120 points in 12 seasons with the Warriors.

Copyright © 1994 Brian Spurlock/Spurlock Photography, Inc.

INDIVIDUAL RECORDS

Career

    Points: 17,783, Wilt Chamberlain, 1959–65

    Rebounds: 12,771, Nate Thurmond, 1963–74

    Assists: 4,855, Guy Rodgers, 1958–66

    Field Goal Pct.: .581, Chris Gatling, 1991–96

    Free Throw Pct.: .896, Rick Barry, 1965–67, 1972–78

Season

    Points: 4,029, Wilt Chamberlain, 1961–62

    Rebounds: 2,149, Wilt Chamberlain, 1960–61

    Assists: 848, Eric Floyd, 1986–87

    Field Goal Pct.: .588, Bernard King, 1980–81

    Free Throw Pct.: .924, Rick Barry, 1977–78

ACROSS

4. Called for an offensive foul
8. Warriors' head coach
10. Column heading on roster (abbr.)
11. Retain possession
12. Before season or game
13. Jog
15. Upstart women's pro league (init.)
17. Traded to Miami with Gatling for Coles and Willis
21. Groups of spectators
22. Downstate rival (init.)
23. Grab a missed shot (abbr.)
25. Up and ___
27. His No. 14 is retired
29. Warriors' 1st round pick in '85 from St. John's
30. Basket
32. Slang for basketball player
34. Head coach of '75 NBA championship team
37. ___ guard
38. Capable
39. Give up
40. Bob Lewis' alma mater (init.)
43. Keep your ___ on the ball.
46. Defunct league with red, white and blue ball (init.)

47. Dunk
48. Stretch prior to a game
49. Warriors' head coach, 1988–95
53. Skein
54. In the vicinity
55. Wear out
56. Was victorious
57. Fastbreak
58. Rests on the bench
59. Column heading on roster (abbr.)

DOWN

1. MVP of '75 NBA Finals
2. Mode of transportation on road trips
3. Larry, Otis, Phil and Derek
5. Stadium
6. Dine
7. 1-pointer (init.)
9. 3-time all-star suspended by NBA for most of 1997–98 season
10. 1st player selected in '93 draft came in trade from Orlando
11. Warriors' coach, 1986–88
14. ___-announcer (init.)

16. Muscle spasm
18. Center acquired from Indiana in Mullin trade
19. The Good Ol' Days: The way it ___.
20. Usual day parts for weekday games
23. Official
24. No game scheduled
26. Tie the score
28. Warriors' career scoring leader
31. Extra period (abbr.)
33. He ___ Game
34. Away
35. No. 42 was a 7-time all-star with the Warriors
36. Deadlock
37. Medium range
39. Period
41. Players' rep on the floor
42. Spectators
44. Payment in Japan league
45. Rim
50. Blatant
51. Basket cords
52. Ricochet
55. End of a foot

Solution on page 180

RETIRED UNIFORM NUMBERS

14	Tom Meschery
16	Alvin Attles
24	Rick Barry
42	Nate Thurmond

```
I  P  H  I  B  W  I  L  K  E  S  U  R  C  L
F  U  L  K  S  H  S  M  G  N  I  K  H  M  L
R  N  R  R  S  N  I  L  L  U  M  A  G  E  O
E  I  R  U  S  S  E  R  L  A  M  S  O  S  R
E  A  O  M  Y  E  S  D  L  B  H  F  T  C  R
Y  E  I  M  S  L  I  O  E  O  E  L  T  H  A
O  T  L  U  I  T  G  R  R  O  M  O  L  E  C
H  A  L  L  I  T  L  T  G  Y  M  Y  I  R  G
N  I  E  L  B  A  S  O  N  A  O  D  E  Y  N
I  U  W  I  I  P  I  L  L  I  H  P  B  E  I
Z  L  E  N  H  A  R  D  A  W  A  Y  G  H  L
I  H  R  T  F  K  L  H  Y  R  R  A  B  Y  T
R  G  P  T  T  O  M  I  S  E  L  R  A  C  A
A  A  S  R  E  G  D  O  R  A  M  L  S  A  G
N  T  H  U  R  M  O  N  D  N  O  S  L  E  N
```

ARIZIN	GOLA	NELSON
ATTLES	GOTTLIEB	RAY
BARRY	HARDAWAY	RODGERS
CARLESIMO	KING	SHORT
CHAMBERLAIN	LEE	SMITH
FLOYD	MESCHERY	SPREWELL
FULKS	MULLIN	THURMOND
GATLING	MULLINS	WILKES

HOUSTON ROCKETS

Since the Rockets came into existence in 1967–68, there have been two names that have been nearly constant: Tomjanovich and Patterson.

Rudy Tomjanovich has either played for (1970–81), scouted for (1981–83) or coached (assistant, 1983–92; head, 1992–98) the Rockets in 28 of their 31 seasons. The five-time all-star is the third-leading scorer in Rockets' history, is one of two players who has had his number retired by the franchise, and is the ninth head coach in club history.

Ray Patterson became president and general manager of the Rockets in 1972 and remained in that capacity until his son, Steve, succeeded him in 1989. Ray earned NBA Executive of the Year honors in 1976–77 and is the only GM in league history to lead two different franchises to the NBA Finals (Milwaukee 1971, Houston 1981 and 1986).

Neither of those two were around, though, when the Rockets began in San Diego. Robert Breitbard purchased an expansion franchise from the NBA in 1968 and began operation that fall as the San Diego Rockets. The first team was coached by Jack McMahon and wound up 15–67. John Block was the leading scorer with 20.2 points a game, followed by Don Kojis (19.7) and Dave Gambee (13.4).

The following year, the Rockets improved to 37–45 and featured a pair of guards who went on to become outstanding NBA coaches—Pat Riley and Rick Adelman. The Rockets rounded out their stay in San Diego with seasons of 27 and 40 wins.

On June 23, 1971, Texas Sports Investments, Inc., a group of civic, business and sports minded figures headed by Bill Goldberg and Wayne Duddleston, purchased the Rockets for $5 million and moved the team to Houston. The Rockets didn't have a permanent home that first season. They played in three different buildings in Houston (Hofheinz Pavilion, the Astrodome and Astrohall) and three other sites around the state (El Paso, San Antonio and Waco).

Over the next five years, the Rockets played just under .500 ball, under two coaches—Tex Winter and John Egan. Tom Nissalke was named the head coach prior to the 1976–77 season. The Rockets also added two key players. John Lucas was the club's first-round draft pick out of Maryland and Moses Malone (who wound up a two-time league MVP as a Rocket) was traded to Houston from Buffalo in the first week of the season for a pair of first-round draft choices. The new faces helped propel the Rockets to a 49–33 record and the Central Division championship. The Rockets beat the Washington Bullets, 4 games to 2, in the first round of the playoffs, but lost in the Eastern Conference finals to Philadelphia, 4–2.

With Tomjanovich out with an injury for most of the season, the Rockets slipped from first place to last with a 28–54 mark in 1977–78. But the following season, they rebounded to 47–35. Nissalke was replaced by Del Harris and the Rockets went 41–41. The 1980–81 season appeared to be more of the same mediocrity when they finished 40–42, and grabbed the final playoff spot by a game. But the Rockets caught on fire in the playoffs. They eliminated the Los Angeles Lakers in the mini-series, 2–1. They defeated the San Antonio Spurs, 4–3, then beat Kansas City, 4–1, to advance to the NBA Finals against the Boston Celtics. Houston put a scare into Boston by winning Game 2 in Beantown, but dropped the championship series, 4–2.

The Rockets showed promise by going 46–36 the next season, but then they fell to an all-time low at 14–68. The disastrous season did have one reward, though. The Rockets won a post-season coin-flip for the No. 1 pick in the college draft, and they selected Virginia's Ralph Sampson. The 7-foot-4 center was named the NBA Rookie of the Year, but the Rockets still couldn't escape the basement of the Western Conference. They won another coin-flip and again had the No. 1 pick in the draft. Houston passed on Michael Jordan and selected local college hero (H)akeem Olajuwon.

With the Twin Towers, the Rockets improved to 48–34, but lost in the opening round of the playoffs. In 1985–86, though, Houston went 51–31 and advanced to the NBA Finals versus Boston. The Celtics again prevailed, 4–2. Sampson was injured the following season and the Twin Towers and the Rockets suffered. They didn't win a division title again until 1992–93. Under rookie coach Tomjanovich, the Rockets finished 55–27 and won the Division title, but lost in the second round of the playoffs to Seattle, 4–3.

Prior to the 1993–94 season, the Rockets were sold to Leslie Alexander, who assembled his fortune as a securities trader on Wall Street. He quickly replaced Steve Patterson as G.M., but made few changes to the player roster. None were needed. The Rockets rolled to a franchise-best 58–24 record and the Midwest Division title. In the playoffs, Houston beat Portland, 3–1, Phoenix, 4–3, and Utah, 4–1, to advance to the NBA Finals against New York. The Rockets fell behind in the series, 3 games to 2, but returned home for Games 6 and 7. The Rockets avoided elimination in Game 6 with an 86–84 win, then won the championship, 90–84.

The following year, the Rockets didn't appear destined to repeat. But a mid-season trade for Clyde Drexler provided a spark. The Rockets finished 47–35, just the sixth best record in the Western Conference. But in the playoffs they overcame the home court disadvantage in every round to win their second straight championship. Houston bounced back from a 2–1 deficit to beat Utah in the opening round, 3–2; it came back from a 3–1 deficit to Phoenix to win the second round, 4–3; it beat San Antonio in the Conference finals, 4–2; then put everything together to blitz Orlando in the Finals, 4–0.

With Olajuwon missing 10 games due to injuries and Drexler 30, the Rockets finished 48–34 in 1995–96. The No. 5 seed upset the L.A. Lakers in the opening round, but then fell to eventual finalist Seattle, 4–0.

The Rockets acquired former league MVP Charles Barkley prior to the 1996–97 season. Houston improved to 57–25 and advanced to the Conference finals before losing to Utah, 4 games to 2.

In 1997–98, Olajuwon missed 35 games, Barkley 14 and Drexler 12. The Rockets, older and ailing, fell to 41–41 and were eliminated in the first round of the playoffs.

Copyright © 1996 Brian Spurlock/Spurlock Photography, Inc.

Hakeem Olajuwon is the Rockets' career leader in points, rebounds and steals.

INDIVIDUAL RECORDS

Career

Points: 24,422, Hakeem Olajuwon, 1984–98

Rebounds: 12,199, Hakeem Olajuwon, 1984–98

Assists: 4,402, Calvin Murphy, 1970–83

Field Goal Pct.: .559, Otis Thorpe, 1988–94

Free Throw Pct.: .941, Rick Barry, 1978–80

Season

Points: 2,520, Moses Malone, 1981–82

Rebounds: 1,444, Moses Malone, 1978–79

Assists: 768, John Lucas, 1977–78

Field Goal Pct.: .592, Otis Thorpe, 1991–92

Free Throw Pct.: .958, Calvin Murphy, 1980–81

ACROSS

1. Move smoothly
4. Type of shot
5. Tips
8. Former home of Kings (init.)
10. Playoff nemesis (init.)
12. ___ Towers
13. Arm joints
14. League MVP in '79 and '82
16. ___ and in
17. Where severely injured players are sent (init.)
19. Extra period (abbr.)
23. Team without the ball
25. Formerly Akeem
26. Logo registration (abbr.)
27. ___ vs. Them
28. 3-of-5, .500 or 34.3 mpg (abbr.)
29. Wire service (init.)
31. Tap
33. Game sphere
35. The Big E
36. ___ trip
38. Publicity (init.)
39. Outscore the opponent
40. A cheer
41. John Lucas' alma mater (init.)
44. ___ and out
45. Midwest, Central, Atlantic and Pacific

47. Boot
48. Smack
49. Rejection (init.)
52. Avery Johnson's alma mater (init.)
55. Fall behind
56. Rockets' career field goal pct. leader
57. Jump ball arc
58. 1st word of the national anthem
60. Older player
62. St. Mary's guard led Rockets in 3-point shooting in 1986–87 and 1987–88
64. Regulations
66. Throws out of the game
67. ___ shoots, he scores!

DOWN

2. Alley-oop passes
3. Low
4. NBA Rookie of the Year in '84
6. Kept on the scoreboard (abbr.)
7. Trades
8. Leg joint
9. Star of the game
11. Rockets' WNBA counterpart

15. Removal from the game by a referee
18. List of players
20. Rudy T
21. Dunk
22. Rockets' career leader in assists
24. Dines
30. U. of Utah guard played with Rockets from 1971–79
31. Journeys
32. ___-announcer (init.)
34. Noisy
37. Stuff
38. Workout
42. Medium range
43. Deadlocks
46. Column heading on roster (abbr.)
50. Take the ball away
51. Swap
53. Painted stripe
54. Make a basket
56. Wear out
59. On fire
60. Against (abbr.)
61. Unnamed opponent (init.)
63. Play ___ or trade me!
65. Former

Solution on page 180

Solution on page 180

RETIRED UNIFORM NUMBERS

23   Calvin Murphy
45   Rudy Tomjanovich

```
D  O  A  R  E  L  I  E  L  E  T  F  A  C  Y
S  L  I  Y  T  R  O  N  O  S  P  M  A  S  E
E  A  T  R  E  N  N  U  K  Y  F  J  Y  R  B
R  J  O  H  N  S  O  N  W  K  U  O  E  D  A
M  U  J  P  O  S  M  A  I  L  L  I  W  H  R
L  W  L  O  S  S  E  N  J  U  D  R  N  C  K
L  O  H  X  N  O  N  S  C  K  I  M  H  I  L
E  N  T  O  E  E  R  A  O  V  A  A  N  V  E
V  W  R  F  R  E  S  J  O  R  Y  Y  C  O  Y
A  E  R  T  L  R  I  E  I  E  N  R  H  N  T
E  C  C  X  A  S  Y  N  S  D  I  R  A  A  D
L  H  E  D  A  J  R  O  Y  P  L  A  N  J  Y
C  R  E  S  W  I  L  L  I  S  W  B  E  M  O
D  E  P  R  O  H  T  A  U  R  E  H  Y  O  L
T  M  U  R  P  H  Y  M  E  D  N  W  F  T  P
```

BARKLEY	JONES	NEWLIN
BARRY	KOJIS	OLAJUWON
CHANEY	KUNNERT	REID
DREXLER	LEAVELL	SAMPSON
ELIE	LUCAS	THORPE
HAYES	MALONE	TOMJANOVICH
HORRY	MARIN	WILLIAMS
JOHNSON	MURPHY	WILLIS

INDIANA PACERS

The Indiana Pacers were one of the original franchises when the American Basketball Association began in the summer of 1967. They also proved to be the most successful. In the nine ABA seasons, the Pacers won three titles, were in the championship series two other times and had the league's best record another season.

Prior to the Pacers, there were two unsuccessful NBA franchises in Indianapolis: the Jets in 1948–49 and the Olympians from 1949–53. So it had been a decade-and-a-half since professional basketball was in the capital city of the basketball hotbed. When word spread that a new league was forming and accepting applications, a group of businessmen in Indiana collected the franchise fee of $6,000 and formed the Pacers. Indiana's first move was to try to lure hometown hero Oscar Robertson away from the NBA. He declined the invitation, but offered one piece of advice, "Get Roger Brown!"

Brown was one of several former college stars who were blackballed by the NBA because of their association with alleged gamblers. He signed in an instant. The Pacers added Freddie Lewis, Bob Netolicky, Reggie Harding and Oliver Darden. They were coached by Larry Staverman and struggled on the court, finishing 38–40. It was in that first season that the Pacers' Jerry Harkness set a record that still stands. He sank a game-winning 88-foot shot, the longest in the history of professional basketball. In the off-season, the Pacers added the ABA's Rookie of the Year, Mel Daniels, in a trade with Minnesota. Indiana started the next season 2–7 and Staverman was replaced by Bob "Slick" Leonard. He turned the Pacers' fortunes around for good. They were 42–27 the rest of the way, won the Eastern Division and advanced to the ABA Finals before losing to Oakland, 4–1. Daniels was the league's MVP, averaging 24.0 points and 16.5 rebounds.

The Pacers went on to win three of the next four championships. In the process they added George McGinnis, Billy Keller and Rick Mount. After their final title in 1972–73, they began a slow decline. They still made it to the Finals in 1974–75, but they went from 51 wins to 46 to 45 to 39. In the final ABA season, the Pacers finished fifth and were eliminated in the first round of the playoffs.

As most of the ABA teams were folding from financial problems, the Pacers were able to remain afloat and were one of four ABA squads that merged into the NBA in the summer of 1976. The price was costly, though. Each team was required to pay a $3.2 million initiation fee. They weren't allowed to share in television revenues for four years (even today, one-seventh of each former ABA team's television money is sent to a former team owner in St. Louis who was not part of the merger) and they were not allowed to participate in the 1976 college draft.

With the franchise in a pinch for money, players were traded for cash and the club's talent pool began to deteriorate. The Pacers were 36–46 in their first NBA season and out of the playoffs for the first time in franchise history. As more players (and their salaries) were discarded, the team won just 31, then 38, then 37 games. In 1979, Sam Nassi bought the Pacers and attempted to bring the Pacers back to respectability. The popular Leonard was replaced prior to the 1980–81 season by Jack McKinney. The Pacers responded to the change and finished 44–38. They made the NBA playoffs for the first time, but were eliminated in two straight games. McKinney was named the NBA Coach of the Year.

McKinney was gone after four years and was replaced by George Irvine. Nassi sold the team in 1983 to Melvin and Herbert Simon, and the brothers infused the club with the necessary capital. Donnie Walsh was named general manager in 1986 and has raised the club to the rank of "title-contending" team. The Pacers hovered around .500 for seven years, despite going through five coaches in eight years. Irvine was replaced by Jack Ramsay in the summer of 1986. Ramsay was gone seven games into the 1988–89 season and was replaced by Daniels, then Irvine, then Dick Versace. Versace stayed on until he was fired in the middle of the 1990–91 season. Bob Hill took over and lasted two-and-a-half years. Larry Brown was hired in the summer of 1993.

The Pacers' fortunes took a turn for the better immediately. Indiana, led by Olympic and all-star guard Reggie Miller, won their final eight regular season games to roll to an NBA club-record 47 wins in 1993–94. The Pacers remained hot in the playoffs, upsetting the Orlando Magic in the first round for the franchise's first NBA series win. They eliminated the conference-champion Atlanta Hawks in the second round and led the New York Knicks, 3–2, in the Eastern Conference finals, before bowing out.

In 1994–95, the Pacers proved they were not a fluke. They went 52–30 and won the Central Division title and again advanced to the seventh game of the Conference finals. This time they lost to Orlando.

In 1995–96, the Pacers matched their club record with 52 wins, but injuries to Miller and center Rik Smits took their toll. The Pacers lost in the opening round of the playoffs to Atlanta. The Pacers slipped to 39–43 in 1996–97 and Brown departed. Enter Larry Bird, a living Hoosier Legend, to make his coaching debut.

Bird led the veteran Pacers squad to a club-record 58–24 mark and earned the NBA Coach of the Year award. The Pacers advanced to the Conference finals for the third time in five years and took the Chicago Bulls to the final minute of Game 7 before bowing out.

Copyright © 1998 Brian Spurlock/Spurlock Photography, Inc.

Reggie Miller has played more games in a Pacers' uniform than anyone in history.

INDIVIDUAL RECORDS

Career

    Points: 17,402, Reggie Miller, 1987–98

    Rebounds: 4,601, Rik Smits, 1988–98

    Assists: 4,038, Vern Fleming, 1984–95

    Field Goal Pct.: .550, Dale Davis, 1991–98

    Free Throw Pct.: .902, John Long, 1986–89

Season

    Points: 2,075, Billy Knight, 1976–77

    Rebounds: 860, Clark Kellogg, 1982–83

    Assists: 713, Mark Jackson, 1997–98

    Field Goal Pct.: .568, Dale Davis, 1992–93

    Free Throw Pct.: .939, Chris Mullin, 1997–98

ACROSS

3. Pacers' head coach
5. Former
6. Defensive specialist acquired in trade with Seattle
9. Cheryl's "little" brother
10. Fastbreak
11. ___-announcer (init.)
12. In and ___
13. Drive: Go to the ___
14. He ___ Game
16. Feeling ill
19. His No. 34 is retired
22. ___ vs. Them

23. College sports' governing body (init.)
24. Begins the game
25. Played in more games than any Pacer
27. Tap
28. Provides gear
30. Take the ball away (abbr.)
32. Led NBA in assists in 1996–97
35. Quinn Buckner's alma mater (init.)
36. Go ___ guy
38. Tom Thacker's alma mater (init.)
39. Before fake or after double

41. Slick
42. Tug
43. Schrempf
45. Grab missed shots (abbr.)
49. Late night talk show host
50. Throw the ball away (abbr.)
53. Dr. Jack
57. Fisticuffs
58. Column heading on roster
60. NBA Coach of the Year in '81
62. Gimme basket
64. Rejection (init.)
65. At
66. Youngest player ever on the cover of Sports Illustrated

DOWN

1. Eddie Johnson's alma mater (init.)
2. Mode of team travel
3. Original Pacer, his No. 35 is retired
4. Carom at other team's basket (init.)
5. Finishes
6. Pacers' home
7. Boot
8. Column heading on roster (abbr.)
9. Big Mac
15. ___-___ record (init.)
17. Roster spot for hurt players (init.)
18. Pass leading to a basket
19. Dale or Antonio
20. Sick
21. The Dunking Dutchman
22. LaSalle Thompson's alma mater (init.)
26. And so forth
29. Pick off a pass (abbr.)
31. Ducats
32. Leaps
33. Purdue guard was 3-point king of ABA
34. Nil
37. Not covered
39. Kept on scoreboard (abbr.)
40. Rick Mount's alma mater (init.)
43. ___ of game
44. Used to wipe off sweat
46. Bob Hill's nickname
47. Logo registration (abbr.)
48. Unsigned player (init.)
51. TV talk: ___, Mom!
52. Toss
54. 3-point line
55. Missouri center was Pacers' 1st round pick in '83 (abbr.)
56. Payment for game in Japan
57. Personal, flagrant or technical
59. Greg Minor's alma mater (init.)
60. Month for playoffs
61. Dine
63. Away
64. Play-___-play announcer

Solution on page 181

RETIRED UNIFORM NUMBERS

30	George McGinnis
34	Mel Daniels
35	Roger Brown

```
A  H  C  I  V  O  N  A  P  I  T  S  N  L  F
M  E  B  S  T  I  M  S  K  E  L  L  O  G  G
M  C  G  I  N  N  I  S  E  N  I  G  S  H  N
E  D  K  W  R  I  O  L  L  R  T  T  R  I  W
L  A  A  E  R  D  E  B  L  S  R  R  E  L  O
L  N  R  V  Y  W  U  M  E  A  B  E  P  L  R
S  I  Y  B  I  S  S  B  R  C  E  H  I  M  B
M  E  K  S  E  S  U  O  E  L  K  C  R  A  G
A  L  G  I  Y  S  E  O  S  A  O  E  A  N  N
I  S  C  H  R  E  M  P  F  N  I  B  D  N  I
L  J  A  C  K  S  O  N  A  N  I  L  L  U  M
L  L  O  I  I  R  M  P  M  A  R  T  C  S  E
I  I  T  H  G  Y  K  C  I  L  O  T  E  N  L
W  K  N  I  G  H  T  D  R  A  N  O  E  L  F
S  I  N  R  E  L  L  I  M  M  A  N  E  L  S
```

BEST	JACKSON	MILLER
BIRD	KELLER	MULLIN
BROWN	KELLOGG	NETOLICKY
BUSE	KNIGHT	PERSON
DANIELS	LEONARD	SCHREMPF
DAVIS	LEWIS	SMITS
FLEMING	MCGINNIS	STIPANOVICH
HILLMAN	MCKEY	WILLIAMS

LOS ANGELES CLIPPERS

The *New York Daily News* headline read: Now it's "Hip to Clip" in L.A.

It wasn't always that way. For years the stepchild to the Lakers in the City of Angels, the Clippers have made strides to reach equal footing with Showtime in the Forum.

The Clippers qualified for the playoffs in 1991–92 and 1992–93, the first playoff appearances since the franchise was in Buffalo 20 years ago. They were back in post-season play in 1996–97.

The Clippers began as the Buffalo Braves in 1970–71 and were sold before they even played a game. Paul Snyder, head of Freezer Queen, purchased the franchise on Oct. 13, 1970, the day prior to the first regular season game. That first team was coached by Dolph Schayes and finished at 22–60. Bob Kauffman (20.4 points per game) and Don May (20.2) were the leading scorers.

The following season Schayes was replaced after losing the first game and John McCarthy took over the rest of the way. That second team also was 22–60. The Braves decided to hire Jack Ramsay as the head coach prior to the 1972–73 season. His first year was a struggle, and the Braves fell to 21–61. But then Ramsay and the Braves brought excitement to northwestern New York for the next three seasons. The Braves acquired Providence's Ernie DiGregorio as the third player chosen in the college draft and forwards Jim McMillian and Gar Heard in trades to go along with all-star Bob McAdoo. All those changes paid off. McAdoo led the NBA in scoring with 30.6 points per game, and the Braves went 42–40, qualifying for their first playoffs.

In 1974–75, McAdoo again led the league in scoring (34.5 ppg) and the Braves improved to 49–33, the third best record in the NBA. However, the Braves faced the Washington Bullets in the Conference semifinals and were eliminated, 4 games to 3. In 1975–76, McAdoo completed a trifecta by leading the league in scoring once more (31.1 ppg) and the Braves finished 46–36. This time they won a mini-series against Philadelphia, 2–1, but lost in the Conference semifinals to the Boston Celtics, 4–2.

There were several changes for the Braves in 1976–77. Prior to the start of the season Ramsay left, and he was replaced by Tates Locke. Then Snyder sold 50 percent of the team to John Y. Brown, the creator of Kentucky Fried Chicken. Twenty games into the season, McAdoo was traded with Tom McMillen to the New York Knicks for John Gianelli and cash. Locke was fired 46 games into the season when the team started 16–30, and Bob MacKinnon and Joe Mullaney shared the coaching duties the rest of the way. Near the end of the season, which finished 30–52, Brown assumed sole ownership of the team. The Kentucky attorney won a title in the American Basketball Association as the owner of the Kentucky Colonels, and he wanted an NBA title, too. His first act as the sole owner was to hire Norm Sonju as the president and general manager. Sonju hired Cotton Fitzsimmons as the coach of the 1977–78 squad which fell even further to 27–55.

It was the summer of 1978 when the Braves were part of one of the most unique trades in the history of professional sports. The club didn't trade a player and it didn't trade a coach. It traded owners. Brown traded the Braves franchise to Irv Levin in exchange for the Boston Celtics. Levin, involved in the motion picture business, wanted to be close to both ventures and moved his new franchise to San Diego. The team now would be called the Clippers. Gone were Sonju and Fitzsimmons. In were Harold Lipton as Executive VP and Gene Shue as coach.

The Clippers' first season in San Diego was a successful one. The team went 43–39 and averaged 9,230 fans a night. In May, 1979, the Clippers got national attention when they signed Bill Walton as a free agent. Walton, who missed the previous season with a foot injury, played out his option with Portland and returned to his hometown area. It was a costly acquisition, though. The Clippers had to compensate the Trail Blazers with Kevin Kunnert, Kermit Washington, a first-round draft pick and cash. Walton played only 169 games for the Clippers over the next six years.

The Clippers began a quick decline and coaches and players began coming and going through a revolving door. The franchise was sold again, this time to Donald Sterling in the summer of 1981. Sterling moved the franchise to Los Angeles in 1984. The Clippers' home was the L.A. Sports Arena on the edge of the Southern Cal campus. The Clippers didn't fare any better in L.A., reaching their lowest point in 1986–87 with a record of 12–70. But Larry Brown was hired as the head coach at mid-season in 1991–92. He guided the Clippers to a mark of 23–12 to finish 45–37 and into their first playoffs since 1976. In 1992–93 the Clippers qualified for the playoffs again at 41–41, but Brown departed, citing differences with the front office. Bob Weiss was named as his replacement.

Weiss' 1993–94 team went 27–55, and he was replaced by the veteran Bill Fitch. The Clippers dropped to 17–65 in 1994–95, but rebounded to 29–53 in 1995–96.

The Clippers have struggled despite 19 first-round draft picks (nearly all of them lottery selections) in the last 12 years. In the summer of 1998, the Clippers had the No. 1 pick in the draft and selected center Michael Olowokandi from Pacific University.

Copyright © 1997 Brian Spurlock/Spurlock Photography, Inc.

Loy Vaught is the Clippers' career rebounding leader.

INDIVIDUAL RECORDS
Career

    Points: 12,735, Randy Smith, 1971–83

    Rebounds: 4,471, Loy Vaught, 1990–98

    Assists: 3,498, Randy Smith, 1971–83

    Field Goal Pct.: .542, Swen Nater, 1977–83

    Free Throw Pct.: .906, Ernie DiGregorio, 1973–77

Season

    Points: 2,831, Bob McAdoo, 1974–75

    Rebounds: 1,216, Swen Nater, 1979–80

    Assists: 914, Norm Nixon, 1983–84

    Field Goal Pct.: .637, James Donaldson, 1984–85

    Free Throw Pct.: .945, Ernie DiGregorio, 1976–77

ACROSS

3. Up and ___

5. Column heading on roster (abbr.)

6. Pick

8. Team nickname in Buffalo

10. Matinee

13. Premiere

15. College sports' governing body (init.)

17. Rest on the bench

20. Do it ___!

22. Clippers' head coach, 1994–98

23. Work of stat crew

24. Section of arena

25. Arm joint

28. Michigan guard had 2,810 assists from 1988–95

29. Tip

31. NBA MVP in 1974–75

33. Play-___-play announcer

35. ___ shoots, he scores!

37. Makes a basket

40. Players' years old

42. Franchise's career scoring leader

43. ___-captain

44. Broadcast vehicle for games (abbr.)

46. T-shirt size

48. Stars of games

49. Charles Outlaw's nickname
51. Dine
53. Franchise's career leader in blocked shots
54. Ricochet
56. Wager on a game
58. Do ___ die
59. S, M or L
61. Ahead: ___ top
62. Roster spot for hurt players (init.)
63. Away
65. ___ vs. Them
66. Point value of FG
67. Foe
68. Dunk

DOWN

1. Contest
2. Play ___ or trade me!
4. Basket cord
5. Signal end of periods
6. Jump, hook or set
7. Throws out of the game
8. Clippers' head coach, 1992–93
9. Clippers' former home
11. 2-pointer
12. Stretch before the game
14. Column heading on roster (abbr.)
16. Hall of Famer Dolph or Danny
18. Treat a sprained ankle
19. Basket
21. ___–___ record (init.)
22. Column heading on stat sheet (init.)
26. Easy shot: ___-up
27. Alex Stivrins' alma mater (init.)
30. Fruit drink
31. Game
32. Ernie D
34. A cheer
36. Set club record with 914 assists in 1983–84
38. NBA's Rookie of the Year in 1982–83
39. Regulation
41. Make a defensive stand
45. Against (abbr.)
47. The paint
49. Nighttime furniture
50. Led NBA in rebounding in 1987–88
52. The lane
55. Double team
56. Game sphere
57. Squad
60. Hotel
64. Last column on box score (init.)
65. Bingo Smith's alma mater (init.)

Solution on page 181

RETIRED UNIFORM NUMBERS
None

```
O  B  G  H  H  D  S  G  N  I  M  M  U  C  D
R  B  E  N  J  A  M  I  N  E  F  G  I  D  I
M  N  H  E  O  Y  X  S  J  R  R  L  N  R  G
A  J  T  T  H  O  F  O  E  E  L  N  T  N  R
N  A  I  X  N  A  H  E  T  I  W  N  H  I  E
N  A  M  H  S  N  S  A  G  O  T  M  G  T  G
I  I  S  A  O  N  N  M  R  A  C  H  U  R  O
N  N  R  O  N  A  S  B  A  Y  C  U  A  A  R
G  S  M  A  I  L  L  I  W  E  F  N  V  M  I
H  J  A  F  G  S  R  N  A  L  T  R  N  S  O
S  W  A  L  T  U  O  P  M  T  R  E  O  A  K
H  R  O  H  C  T  I  F  E  N  N  P  G  Y  T
U  K  O  N  L  E  N  G  H  A  E  R  E  E  V
E  R  A  A  L  L  N  O  S  D  L  A  N  O  D
B  L  W  M  C  A  D  O  O  D  K  H  I  G  S
```

BENJAMIN	FREE	NIXON
BROWN	GRANT	OUTLAW
CAGE	HARPER	RAMSAY
CUMMINGS	JOHNSON	SHUE
DANTLEY	MANNING	SMITH
DIGREGORIO	MARTIN	VAUGHT
DONALDSON	MCADOO	WALTON
FITCH	NATER	WILLIAMS

LOS ANGELES LAKERS

Magic Johnson. Jerry West. Wilt Chamberlain. Kareem Abdul-Jabbar. Those were the greats that gave Los Angeles six NBA titles. But George Mikan, Vern Mikkelsen, Jim Pollard and Slater Martin were the greats that won five NBA titles in Minneapolis that made the Lakers the great franchise that it is today.

How Mikan, a 6-foot-10 giant with thick glasses, even became a Laker is bizarre. Mikan completed his collegiate career at DePaul in 1946 and signed immediately with his hometown Chicago American Gears team of the National Basketball League. It was too late in the season for him to play in anything but the post-season world professional tournament where he scored 100 points in five games and was selected the tourney's MVP. Big No. 99 sat out the first six weeks of the following season in a contract dispute, but finally began playing for the Gears. He led them to the NBL title and a dynasty was in the making. The following summer, Gears owner Maurice White envisioned his own 24-team league. He would own all of the teams and arenas and call it the Professional Basketball League of America. The PBLA collapsed in the first month of operation and the Gears' players were distributed among the NBL squads. Mikan was awarded to a first-year team, the Minneapolis Lakers. Mikan led the Lakers to the NBL title. The Lakers then joined three other teams in jumping to the rival Basketball Association of America, which eventually evolved into the NBA.

The Lakers were an instant impact, winning the 1948–49 title. With John Kundla as the head coach, the Lakers were the dominant franchise, winning five titles in their first six seasons. Mikan called it quits as a player following the 1955–56 season and the Lakers struggled for the remainder of the decade.

The team moved to Los Angeles in the summer of 1960. It was also that summer when the club used its No. 1 draft pick to select West Virginia guard Jerry West. Fred Schaus was named the head coach.

West joined veterans Elgin Baylor, Frank Selvy and "Hot Rod" Hundley, and the Lakers went 36–43 in their first season on the west coast. The next year they added Rudy LaRusso, and the Lakers began a run which saw them make the NBA Finals in nine of the next 12 years.

It was the 1971–72 championship squad that many claim was the greatest NBA team of all time. It won a then-record 69 games, including a pro-sports record 33 straight. Gail Goodrich scored 25.9 points per game; West led the league with 9.7 assists a game (in addition to scoring 25.8 ppg); Wilt Chamberlain led the NBA in rebounds with 19.2 a game; and Bill Sharman was named Coach of the Year.

The following season, the Lakers won 60 games, but lost to the New York Knicks in the NBA Finals. In 1973–74, Chamberlain retired, but the Lakers still won the Pacific Division with a record of 47–35. They were eliminated in the first round of the playoffs. In 1974–75, West retired and Cazzie Russell was injured. The Lakers missed the playoffs for the first time in 14 seasons, going 30–52. In the summer of 1975 the Lakers made a bold move. They orchestrated a trade which brought the game's most dominant player, Kareem Abdul-Jabbar, to Los Angeles. The Lakers had to give up Elmore Smith, Brian Winters, Dave Meyers and Junior Bridgeman.

Abdul-Jabbar was named the league's MVP in 1975–76, but the Lakers won just 40 games and were eliminated in the first round of the playoffs. In 1976–77, Abdul-Jabbar was again the MVP and under new Head Coach West, the Lakers went 53–29. But L.A. was beaten by Portland in the Western Conference finals. The next two seasons the Lakers slipped to 45 and 47 wins and the team was sold to Jerry Buss. West was bumped into the front office and Jack McKinney was named the head coach. But it was the drafting of Earvin "Magic" Johnson with the No. 1 pick (which the Lakers had acquired from the Jazz in exchange for Goodrich in 1976) that made the biggest impact.

McKinney had a bicycle accident and was replaced by Paul Westhead as coach 13 games into the season. The team responded by going 60–22 and winning the NBA championship. Abdul-Jabbar was again the league MVP; Johnson was Rookie of the Year and the playoff MVP. The following year Johnson missed 45 games with a knee injury and the Lakers fell to 54–28 and were eliminated in the first round of the playoffs.

In 1981–82, the Lakers got off to a slow start and Pat Riley replaced Westhead as coach. "Showtime" had arrived. Riley let Johnson lead, and the Lakers went 57–25 and won another NBA title. In the next nine seasons, the Lakers won three championships and were runners-up four other times. But it all came tumbling down on Nov. 7, 1992, when Johnson announced his premature retirement, because he tested positive for the HIV virus. With their stars falling, the Lakers won 43 games in 1991–92, 39 in 1992–93 and 33 in 1993–94 (despite a stint as head coach by Johnson).

Del Harris took over the coaching reins in 1994–95 and helped lead the Lakers back to respectability. L.A. was 48–34 and advanced to the second round of the playoffs. In 1995–96, Johnson returned to the court, this time as a forward. He appeared in 32 games, averaging 14.6 points, 5.7 rebounds and 6.9 assists per game. The rerun of "Showtime," though not as shiny as the original, was still successful. The Lakers were 53–29, but were upset by Houston in the opening round of the playoffs. Johnson announced his retirement—this time for good—following the season. But the Lakers didn't waste any time in getting another superstar, signing free agent Shaquille O'Neal to a reported seven-year, $120 million contract.

Shaq helped lead the Lakers to a 56–26 mark in 1996–97, but the Lakers were beaten in the second round of the playoffs. In 1997–98, the Lakers were 61–21 and advanced to the Conference finals before losing to the Jazz.

Kobe Bryant is the youngest person to play in an NBA All-Star Game.

INDIVIDUAL RECORDS

Career

Points: 25,192, Jerry West, 1960–74

Rebounds: 11,463, Elgin Baylor, 1958–72

Assists: 10,141, Earvin Johnson, 1979–91, 1995–96

Field Goal Pct.: .605, Wilt Chamberlain, 1968–73

Free Throw Pct.: .877, Cazzie Russell, 1974–77

Season

Points: 2,719, Elgin Baylor, 1962–63

Rebounds: 1,712, Wilt Chamberlain, 1968–69

Assists: 989, Earvin Johnson, 1990–91

Field Goal Pct.: .727, Wilt Chamberlain, 1972–73

Free Throw Pct.: .911, Earvin Johnson, 1988–89

ACROSS

1. Was ahead
4. MVP of '88 NBA Finals
6. Easy shot
10. Regulation
12. Nick Van Exel's alma mater (init.)
14. 1st word of the national anthem
16. Won Cable Ace Award as host of Nickelodeon show
18. Stretch
20. Bucket
21. Deadlock
22. Take away the ball (abbr.)
23. Computation of stat crew

24. Double team
26. All right
29. Column heading on roster
31. Center on team that won record 33 straight games
32. 1-on-1
33. Guard was the Atlantic 10 Player of the Year at Temple in '94
35. Point value of FT
36. Long narrow strip of leather
39. Team physician (abbr.)
40. T-shirt size (abbr.)
41. Lakers' career rebounding leader
42. Night before a game
44. Rejection (init.)

45. Located further inside
48. Lakers' head coach, 1981–90
50. Tip
52. Type of shot
53. Great Western ___
55. Bottom half of a uniform
57. Byron Scott's alma mater (init.)
60. Throw the ball away (abbr.)
62. Makes a basket
63. Mode of transportation for team
64. No game scheduled
65. Minneapolis all-star was 1st dominant big man in NBA
66. ___ shoots, he scores!
67. A quarter
70. Cliff Robinson's alma mater (init.)
72. Unnamed opponent (init.)
73. Carom at own basket (init.)
74. Against (abbr.)
75. Extra period (abbr.)

DOWN

2. Where severely injured players are sent (init.)
3. Slams
4. Lakers' career scoring leader
5. Column heading on roster (abbr.)
7. At
8. Doug Christie's alma mater (init.)
9. Alley-oop passes
11. Stadium
13. Assistant coach's tool
15. Cap

17. Formerly Alcindor
19. Lakers' head coach
25. Guard traded to Denver in '98
26. Off the court (init.)
27. Erickson and Owens
28. Tap
30. Left-handed guard has his No. 25 retired
31. NBA's Defensive Player of the Year in 1986–87
34. Tied
37. ___-announcer (init.)
38. Participate
43. Strives for victory
44. Chick Hearn: play-___-play announcer
46. Boston's time zone (init.)
47. Sit on the bench
49. Former
50. Used to mop off sweat
51. Bob Sims' alma mater (init.)
54. Had 138 career triple-doubles, most in NBA history
55. Teams
56. Tumbles
58. Utilize
59. ___ or die
61. Not covered
64. Wager on a game
68. Roster spot for hurt players (init.)
69. Go ___ guy
70. ___ vs. Them
71. ___-captain

Solution on page 182

RETIRED UNIFORM NUMBERS

13	Wilt Chamberlain	33	Kareem Abdul-Jabbar
22	Elgin Baylor	42	James Worthy
25	Gail Goodrich	44	Jerry West
32	Magic Johnson		

```
I  J  S  E  K  L  I  W  B  A  Y  L  O  R  V
W  O  R  T  H  Y  E  L  L  L  E  S  S  U  R
W  H  I  K  I  S  H  M  O  W  I  R  N  L  C
W  N  U  J  T  M  N  O  V  N  N  E  T  A  O
U  S  G  T  H  H  A  C  E  A  X  J  O  R  N
C  O  O  P  E  R  M  E  L  E  O  P  D  U  I
N  N  O  R  E  Y  R  L  L  N  E  S  W  S  A
E  I  D  G  E  G  A  E  E  R  N  V  T  S  L
S  W  R  L  M  E  H  S  T  B  L  A  S  O  R
T  E  I  A  B  S  S  L  T  A  B  B  K  R  E
N  R  C  M  C  I  E  G  E  O  K  J  W  I  B
A  C  H  O  R  K  U  N  D  L  A  I  S  C  M
Y  H  T  R  C  K  O  D  R  A  L  L  O  P  A
R  T  A  R  A  B  B  A  J  L  U  D  B  A  H
B  H  L  E  X  E  N  A  V  R  O  L  Y  A  C
```

ABDUL-JABBAR	JOHNSON	RILEY
BAYLOR	JONES	RUSSELL
BRYANT	KUNDLA	SCOTT
CHAMBERLAIN	LARUSSO	SHARMAN
COOPER	LOVELLETTE	VAN EXEL
GOODRICH	MIKAN	WEST
GREEN	O'NEAL	WILKES
HARRIS	POLLARD	WORTHY

MIAMI HEAT

It started as a germ of an idea in the minds of long-time friends and NBA executives Billy Cunningham and Lewis Schaffel. They wanted to build an NBA team from the ground up. They set their sites on Miami and added three partners new to basketball: theatrical producer Zev Bufman, entertainer Julio Iglesias and cruise lines owner Micky Arison.

That group saw their efforts culminate in the awarding of an NBA franchise on Apr. 22, 1987. The Miami Heat would begin play in 1988–89, along with the Charlotte Hornets.

The first order of business was selecting players. In the expansion draft, each NBA team was allowed to protect eight players. The Heat and Hornets would alternately choose any roster players not protected. The Heat had the first pick. They spent a great deal of time analyzing all of the possibilities and selected Arvid Kramer from Dallas. Arvid who? Arvid Kramer had been selected by the Mavericks in the 1980 expansion draft after playing just eight games for the Denver Nuggets. Kramer never played for the Mavericks (or anyone else in the NBA after that), so he was still on the Mavericks' eligible "roster."

As the fans in Miami were wondering about the Heat's brain trust, Cunningham explained that the Heat, by selecting Kramer, also obtained Dallas' first-round pick in the upcoming college draft. The Mavericks wanted to protect the other veteran players on their active roster and offered the Heat that pick in the college draft to avoid losing Bill Wennington, Uwe Blab or Steve Alford.

The rest of the expansion draft wasn't as difficult to figure out. The Heat picked up ready-to-play veterans Billy Thompson, Fred Roberts, Scott Hastings and Jon Sundvold. They also acquired Kevin Williams, Hansi Gnad, Darnell Valentine, Dwayne Washington, Andre Turner, Conner Henry and John Stroeder.

A week later the Heat selected Syracuse's Rony Seikaly in the college draft (ninth overall pick), DePaul's Kevin Edwards (with the No. 1 pick from Dallas) and Eastern Michigan's Grant Long.

Ron Rothstein, an assistant coach with the Detroit Pistons, was named the Heat's first head coach on July 11, 1988. His assistants were Dave Wohl and Tony Fiorentino.

The Heat lost their opening game, at home against the Los Angeles Clippers, 111–91. The starting line-up for the first game was: Rory Sparrow (a free agent who the Heat signed the week before the season started), Edwards, Seikaly, Pat Cummings (a free agent signee) and Thompson. They were 0–17 before they finally won, beating the Clippers in L.A., 89–88, on Dec. 14. The Heat limped home with a 15–67 record. Besides the season-opening 17-game losing streak, the Heat also had losing streaks of 10 games, 7 (twice), 6, 5 and 4 (twice). They did have a 3-game winning streak in March.

Edwards led a balanced scoring attack with 13.8 points per game. Rory Sparrow (12.5 ppg), Grant Long (11.9 ppg), Seikaly (10.9 ppg), Thompson (10.8 ppg) and Sundvold (10.4 ppg) were also in double-figures.

The Heat selected Michigan's Glen Rice with their No. 1 pick (4th overall) and Syracuse's Sherman Douglas in the 1989 college draft. They saw their record improve slightly to 18–64.

In 1990–91, Miami added Willie Burton through the draft and the young players began to develop. The Heat went 24–58. But Rothstein resigned at the end of the season and was replaced by Kevin Loughery.

The Heat selected Michigan State's Steve Smith in the 1991 college draft. It was Cunningham's plan to build the franchise with young players and look to the future. With Smith, the Heat's top six players all were drafted by Miami from the college ranks. It was up to Loughery to get them to play together.

He did. In 1991–92, the Heat jumped out to a 7–3 record. They lost eight of their next nine games, but they stayed close to .500 the rest of the season. The Heat won four of their last six games to finish at 38–44 and became the first of the recent expansion teams to qualify for the playoffs.

The Heat drew a difficult opponent in the playoffs, the defending champion (and eventual champion) Chicago Bulls. The Heat didn't play well in the first two games in Chicago and were beaten badly in both. But the third game was played in The Miami Arena where the Heat was 28–13 in the regular season. Miami played the Bulls close, but lost down the stretch, 119–114.

The Heat added Southern Cal's Harold Miner in the 1992 college draft and all of southern Florida was looking forward to the 1992–93 season. But injuries to Smith, Edwards and Burton hurt the Heat's chances. They fell to 36–46 and failed to make the playoffs.

Miami did return to the playoffs in 1993–94 after finishing 42–40, but were eliminated in the first round by the Atlanta Hawks, 3–2. In 1994–95, Loughery was replaced by Alvin Gentry midway through the season. The Heat wound up 32–50 and were in search of a savior.

The savior was hoped to be new Head Coach Pat Riley. His controversial hiring prompted many changes to the player roster. Those changes continued throughout the season. The Heat wound up using 22 players en route to a 42–40 record and the final playoff spot in the Eastern Conference. Finishing the season for the Heat were key players Alonzo Mourning, guards Tim Hardaway and Rex Chapman, and forwards Walt Williams, Chris Gatling and Kurt Thomas. Unfortunately, Miami drew Chicago in the first round of the playoffs and the Heat was swept, 3–0.

More roster changes resulted in the Heat finishing 61–21 in 1996–97. They advanced to the Eastern Conference finals before losing to the eventual champion Chicago Bulls, 4 games to 1. Miami repeated as division champ in 1997–98 with a 55–27 mark, but Riley and the Heat were upset in the opening round of the playoffs by the Knicks.

Tim Hardaway was a first-team all-NBA selection in 1997.

INDIVIDUAL RECORDS
Career
Points: 9,248, Glen Rice, 1989–95

Rebounds: 4,544, Rony Seikaly, 1988–94

Assists: 1,946, Bimbo Coles, 1990–96

Field Goal Pct.: .500, Sherman Douglas, 1989–92

Free Throw Pct.: .835, Glen Rice, 1989–95

Season
Points: 1,831, Glen Rice, 1994–95

Rebounds: 934, Rony Seikaly, 1991–92

Assists: 695, Tim Hardaway, 1996–97

Field Goal Pct.: .574, Matt Geiger, 1993–94

Free Throw Pct.: .880, Glen Rice, 1993–94

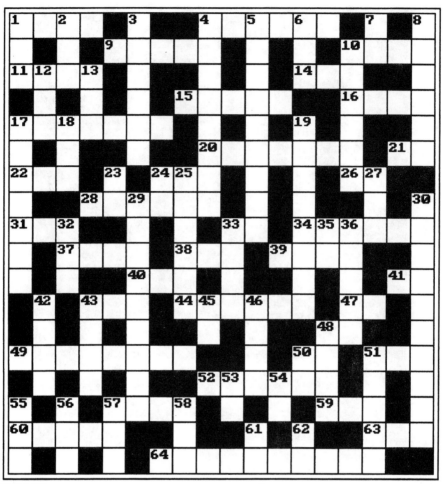

ACROSS

1. Part of FTA
4. Clock keepers
9. Area for subs
10. Heat's career scoring leader
11. Basket cords
14. Type of x ray (init.)
15. Intelligent
16. 1st player to appear in all 82 games for Heat
17. Grab a missed shot
20. Heat's career rebounding leader
21. Do ___ die
22. In and ___

24. .500 record: much ___ about nothing
26. Take away the ball (abbr.)
28. Minnesota swingman chosen in the 1st round in '90
31. Hotel
33. Rejection (init.)
34. Ike
37. Defeat
38. Dream Team: Team ___
39. Cross training exercise
40. Smack
41. ___ shoots, he scores!
43. Mode of team transportation from hotel to arena

44. Heat player chosen by Toronto in '95 expansion draft
47. Throw the ball away (abbr.)
48. 1st word of the national anthem
49. Heat head coach, 1991–95
50. Kevin Edwards' alma mater (init.)
51. Whirlpool
52. Yells
57. Ignore
59. Point value of FG
60. Dribble hard to the basket
63. A team color
64. Number of fans in the stands

DOWN

1. Spectator
2. Time zone for Miami (init.)
3. Guard
4. Louisville forward chosen from Lakers in '88 expansion draft
5. Zo and family
6. Basket
7. TV talk: ___, Mom!
8. Center shipped to Charlotte as part of Mourning trade
10. Heat head coach and family
12. Night before a game
13. Sold out crowd (init.)
17. 1st year players
18. Swat
19. Writes MEE on sneakers in memory of his grandmother
23. Todd Mitchell's alma mater (init.)
24. Away
25. Breakfast food
27. NBA's cable network
29. Heat's 1st head coach
30. Without a loss
32. NBA's TV network
33. Game sphere
35. Kevin Gamble's alma mater (init.)
36. Michigan St. guard drafted in 1st round in '91
42. Basket
43. Equipment carriers
45. Stomach muscle (abbr.)
46. Arrive after the start
48. Eliminate
50. Team physician (abbr.)
51. Make a basket
53. Column heading on roster (abbr.)
54. Former
55. Computation for stat crew
56. Tap
57. Type of shot
58. Wager on a game
61. ___ and out
62. ___-announcer (init.)

Solution on page 182

RETIRED UNIFORM NUMBERS

None

```
N  R  H  Y  U  I  O  S  D  R  A  W  D  E  W
L  O  U  G  H  E  R  Y  S  I  C  O  O  I  D
T  T  H  O  M  P  S  O  N  M  U  O  L  R  O
G  H  S  H  D  N  D  R  A  N  E  L  E  D  U
N  S  M  S  C  A  N  M  L  N  I  N  Y  E  G
I  T  O  P  K  I  W  A  O  S  I  N  L  W  L
R  E  A  W  N  S  S  S  M  M  I  Y  I  T  A
S  I  B  W  E  S  E  I  E  Y  E  L  L  A  S
Y  N  C  R  A  N  T  I  T  L  O  R  R  C  B
L  O  R  E  V  H  S  S  I  N  O  E  N  R  Y
A  U  S  T  I  N  S  R  G  A  G  C  O  R  E
K  H  O  S  M  A  I  L  L  I  W  W  T  I  L
I  M  N  A  O  E  S  F  E  H  N  Y  R  D  L
E  S  U  R  N  E  T  G  N  I  N  R  U  O  M
S  H  A  R  D  A  W  A  Y  O  V  D  B  U  O
```

AUSTIN	LENARD	ROTHSTEIN
BROWN	LONG	SALLEY
BURTON	LOUGHERY	SEIKALY
COLES	MINER	SHAW
DOUGLAS	MOURNING	SMITH
EDWARDS	OWENS	THOMPSON
GEIGER	RICE	WILLIAMS
HARDAWAY	RILEY	WILLIS

MILWAUKEE BUCKS

The entire history of the Milwaukee Bucks' franchise rests on the toss of one coin. Heads or tails. Tails I win; heads I lose. As simple as that. It all happened Mar. 19, 1969.

The Bucks had just completed their first year in the NBA with a record of 27–55. They finished last in the Eastern Division. That first unit included Flynn Robinson, Jon McGlocklin, Lennie Chappell and Wayne Embry. The Phoenix Suns, also completing their first season, finished 16–66 and in last place in the Western Division. As was the rule, the last place team in each division met for a coin-toss to decide which would have the No. 1 pick in that spring's college draft. At stake? UCLA's Lew Alcindor (who changed his name to Kareem Abdul-Jabbar in 1971).

Phoenix, by having the worse record, got to make the call. NBA Commissioner Walter Kennedy flipped the coin. The Suns called heads. The coin came up tails. Milwaukee had the No. 1 pick and selected Alcindor. The Suns, with the second pick in the draft, chose Florida's Neal Walk. Abdul-Jabbar retired after 20 years with an NBA-record 38,387 points. Walk played eight solid years in the NBA for three teams and scored 7,157 points.

The addition of Alcindor gave the Bucks a new look instantly. With Larry Costello as the head coach, they went 56–26 and had the second best record in the league. Alcindor was second in the NBA in scoring (28.8 points per game) and third in rebounding (14.5 per game). The Bucks won their opening playoff series over Philadelphia, but bowed to eventual champion New York in the Eastern Division finals.

Following the season, the Bucks traded Robinson and Charlie Paulk to Cincinnati for all-pro Oscar Robertson, and Don Smith was traded to Seattle for Bob Boozer and Lucius Allen. The Bucks rolled to a 66–16 record, including an NBA-record 20-game winning streak (later broken). Alcindor led the league in scoring (31.7 ppg) and was named the MVP. Milwaukee beat San Francisco, 4 games to 1, in the first round of the playoffs, and the Los Angeles Lakers, 4–1, in the Conference finals. When the Bucks won the NBA Finals, 4–0, over the Baltimore Bullets, it marked just the second time in league history that the Finals were won in a sweep.

In 1971–72, Abdul-Jabbar repeated his scoring and MVP titles and the Bucks went 63–19. But they lost to the Lakers in the Conference finals, 4–2. The Bucks went on to win five straight division titles, culminating in 1973–74. With Abdul-Jabbar again winning MVP honors, the Bucks advanced to the NBA Finals, losing to the Celtics, 4–3.

The next year Abdul-Jabbar missed the first 16 games with a broken hand, and the Bucks were only 3–13. They wound up 38–44 and out of the playoffs. Then on June 16, 1975, the Bucks executed one of the biggest trades in NBA history. They sent Abdul-Jabbar and reserve center Walt Wesley to the Los Angeles Lakers in exchange for Elmore Smith, Brian Winters, Dave Meyers and Junior Bridgeman. Despite the absence of Abdul-Jabbar, the Bucks still went on to win the Midwest Division, but lost in the opening round of the playoffs.

Just 18 games into the 1976–77 season, Costello resigned and assistant Don Nelson took over. That squad fell to 30–52, but the Bucks rebounded the following season with a mark of 44–38. A back injury to Meyers for the entire 1978–79 season dropped the Bucks to 38–44. Milwaukee was struggling in 1979–80 when they acquired Bob Lanier from the Detroit Pistons at the all-star break in exchange for Kent Benson and a first-round draft pick. The Bucks went 20–6 the rest of the way and won the Midwest Division title.

They went on to win seven straight division titles, averaging 55 wins a season. Yet, they never made it to the NBA Finals again.

After an injury-plagued 50–32 season in 1986–87, Nelson departed and was replaced by Del Harris. The Bucks fell to 42–40, then went 49–33 in 1988–89. It was that year that the Bucks moved out of the tiny Milwaukee Arena (with a capacity of 11,052) and into the spacious Bradley Center (with a capacity of 18,633). The Bucks remained competitive, going 44–38 in 1989–90 and 48–34 in 1990–91. Then in 1991–92, Harris was fired when the team got off to an 8–9 start; the Bucks were 23–42 the rest of the way under Frank Hamblen.

On May 12, 1992, former Buck Mike Dunleavy, then the head coach of the Lakers, signed an eight-year contract to be Milwaukee's head coach and VP of basketball operations. The Bucks used 19 different players in 1992–93 and suffered through a 28–54 season, the first time Milwaukee was last in a division since their inaugural season. The Bucks sought help in the draft and got Vin Baker, a future all-star.

Milwaukee remained in the cellar in 1993–94 with a 20–62 record, but their luck prevailed again in the draft lottery. The Bucks were rewarded with the first pick in the 1994 college draft and selected the College Player of the Year, Glen Robinson of Purdue. The Bucks improved to 34–48, but still missed the playoffs. Then following a 25–57 record in 1995–96, Dunleavy gave up his coaching duties. He was replaced on the bench by Chris Ford.

The Bucks improved to 33–49 in 1996–97. Prior to the 1997–98 season Baker was shipped to Seattle as part of a three-team deal. The Bucks received Cleveland's Terrell Brandon and Tyrone Hill.

Milwaukee finished 36–46, then used a draft day trade to acquire Michigan's Robert Traylor. Prior to the start of the 1998–99 season, Ford was fired and replaced on the sidelines by veteran coach George Karl.

Copyright © 1995 Brian Spurlock/Spurlock Photography, Inc.

Glenn Robinson has averaged more than 20 points a game in each of his four seasons.

INDIVIDUAL RECORDS

Career

 Points: 14,211, Kareem Abdul-Jabbar, 1969–75

 Rebounds: 7,161, Kareem Abdul-Jabbar, 1969–75

 Assists: 3,272, Paul Pressey, 1982–90

 Field Goal Pct.: .547, Kareem Abdul-Jabbar, 1969–75

 Free Throw Pct.: .884, Jack Sikma, 1986–91

Season

 Points: 2,822, Kareem Abdul-Jabbar, 1971–72

 Rebounds: 1,346, Kareem Abdul-Jabbar, 1971–72

 Assists: 668, Oscar Robertson, 1970–71

 Field Goal Pct.: .577, Kareem Abdul-Jabbar, 1970–71

 Free Throw Pct.: .922, Jack Sikma, 1987–88

ACROSS

1. Bucks' career scoring leader
6. Throw the ball away (abbr.)
9. At the Bradley Center
10. Fastbreak
11. Make a move: ___ and bake
12. Indiana center was No. 1 pick in '77 draft
13. ___ or die
15. Play ___ or trade me!
17. Bucks head coach, 1987–91
18. Bob Greacen's alma mater (init.)
19. Purdue forward was No. 1 pick in '94 draft
23. Extra period (abbr.)
25. Away
26. 24-years-___
27. Ken Norman's nickname
30. A cheer
31. His No. 4 is retired
33. ___ shoots, he scores!
34. Yell
36. Brad Lohaus' alma mater (init.)
37. A cheer
38. Theodore Edwards' nickname
39. Blackman's nickname
43. Longtime U.S. Olympic basketball coach

46. Has played more games than any other Buck
48. Bucks' career leader in steals
51. Follow
52. Bucks' head coach for '71 championship team
53. Go ___ guy
54. Pool stick
56. No game scheduled
60. Bucks' head coach, 1976–87
62. Simple
63. Scott May's alma mater (init.)
65. Organized yellers on sidelines

DOWN

2. Norfolk St. forward on championship team
3. George, Marques or Mickey
4. Bucks' leading scorer in 1995–96 was traded to Seattle
5. The Big O
6. Height of basket in feet
7. Usual day off (abbr.)
8. Wager on a game
9. Signals end of the period
14. Carom at own basket (init.)
16. Column heading on roster (abbr.)
17. Kareem's Sky ___

20. Roster spot for hurt players (init.)
21. Take the ball away (abbr.)
22. Do it ___!
24. Wraps an ankle
28. Former all-star turned team announcer
29. Monetary penalty
32. Go ___ it!
33. TV talk: ___, Mom!
34. ___-captain
35. Precipitation
40. Off the court (init.)
41. All-star guard part of Abdul-Jabbar trade to Lakers
42. Show it again on TV
44. Stomach muscle (abbr.)
45. Basket cord
46. Part of BS
47. 3-pt. lines
49. Alton Lister's alma mater (init.)
50. Skip pass
55. Utilizes
57. Keep your ___ on the ball
58. Qtr.
59. Deadlock
61. Night before a game
64. Sidney Moncrief's alma mater (init.)

Solution on page 183

RETIRED UNIFORM NUMBERS

1	Oscar Robertson	16	Bob Lanier
2	Junior Bridgeman	32	Brian Winters
4	Sidney Moncrief	33	Kareem Abdul-Jabbar
14	Jon McGlocklin		

```
C  R  O  R  E  S  G  N  I  M  M  U  C  A  R
R  O  B  E  R  T  S  O  N  A  K  E  R  B  D
S  B  S  L  B  B  A  S  A  L  G  U  O  D  A
R  R  H  T  A  A  I  I  P  R  H  E  U  U  N
E  I  U  N  E  L  K  I  H  A  R  N  J  L  D
T  D  M  I  Y  L  E  E  R  T  L  O  E  J  R
N  G  P  E  A  R  L  R  R  E  H  D  A  A  I
I  E  H  R  C  U  I  O  A  N  R  M  R  B  Y
W  M  R  E  H  S  N  V  S  O  K  E  D  B  E
N  A  I  H  R  E  Y  O  F  I  I  D  R  A  S
O  N  E  N  T  I  N  O  S  N  I  B  O  R  S
S  E  S  E  G  D  O  H  A  L  L  E  N  K  E
L  I  E  R  C  E  A  L  R  E  U  E  R  B  R
E  C  I  N  N  I  L  K  C  O  L  G  C  M  P
N  D  R  F  E  I  R  C  N  O  M  N  E  R  A
```

ABDUL-JABBAR	DUNLEAVY	MONCRIEF
ALLEN	FORD	NELSON
BAKER	HARRIS	PIERCE
BREUER	HODGES	PRESSEY
BRIDGEMAN	HUMPHRIES	ROBERTSON
COSTELLO	JOHNSON	ROBINSON
CUMMINGS	LANIER	SIKMA
DOUGLAS	MCGLOCKLIN	WINTERS

MINNESOTA TIMBERWOLVES

In their first two years of existence, the Minnesota Timberwolves totaled more wins than any of the other three expansion teams of their era. After a five-year downslide, the Timberwolves' future is among the brightest.

In the Timberwolves' inaugural season of 1989–90, they went 22–60. Miami and Charlotte, which already had played a season, won 18 and 19 games, respectively. The other new entry, Orlando, won 18. Then in 1990–91, Minnesota went 29–53. Orlando won 31 games, Charlotte 26 and Miami 24. But in 1991–92, the Timberwolves managed just 15 wins and have showed just minor improvement in every season since. They won 19 games the following year, then 20, 21 and finally 26 in 1995–96.

So, what happened? Here's a look from the start:

The state of Minnesota and the city of Minneapolis began as early as 1984 looking at the possibility of getting an NBA franchise. The state had been represented in the NBA from 1948–60 by the Minneapolis Lakers, but that team moved to friendlier confines in Los Angeles. There also were teams in the short-lived American Basketball Association. The Minnesota Muskies played in 1967–68 and the Minnesota Pipers from 1968–70. But major league basketball had been absent from the Twin Cities for quite some time.

On Jan. 12, 1984, Minnesota Governor Rudy Perpich appointed a 30-member task force, chaired by former NBA and Minneapolis Lakers great, George Mikan. Two years later the Governor and Mikan went to league headquarters in New York with $100,000 and an application for entry into the NBA. On Oct. 20, 1986, business partners Harvey Ratner and Marv Wolfenson and attorney Bob Stein attended a league meeting to make a formal proposal. Not waiting for an official announcement, the task force sought a nickname for the team and held a state-wide contest. More than 6,000 entries suggested 1,284 different names with the top two being "Timberwolves" and "Polars." In a run-off, Timberwolves won by a 2-to-1 margin. On Feb. 20, 1987, the Minneapolis City Council approved a plan for a new downtown arena (The Target Center), but it wasn't completed until the 1990–91 NBA season. Until that time, the Timberwolves had to play in the H. H. Humphrey Metrodome. On Apr. 3, 1987, the expansion committee voted to award a franchise to Minnesota, and on Apr. 22 the owners made it official. The price? $32.5 million. But the Timberwolves didn't begin playing for two more years.

In the meantime, they named Stein the team president and Bill Musselman the first head coach. On June 15, 1989, they took part in the expansion draft. Each team was allowed to protect eight players and the Timberwolves and

Orlando Magic took turns selecting players from the remaining players on the roster. No team could lose more than one player. The Timberwolves came out of the draft with a good corps of veterans: Rick Mahorn, Tyrone Corbin, Steve Johnson, Brad Lohaus, David Rivers, Mark Davis, Scott Roth, Shelton Jones, Eric White, Maurice Martin and Gunther Behnke. Then two weeks later, Minnesota participated in its first college draft and selected UCLA guard Pooh Richardson with the 10th overall pick. Missouri center Gary Leonard and Villanova guard Doug West were selected in the second round.

On Oct. 6, 1989, the Timberwolves began their first training camp in nearby Bloomington, Minn. Mahorn was a no-show, so Minnesota traded him to Philadelphia for three future draft picks. The season began Nov. 3. The Timberwolves lost their opener at Seattle, 106–94. The opening day line-up was: Sam Mitchell, Tod Murphy, Lohaus, Tony Campbell and Sidney Lowe. Mitchell scored the first basket. The Timberwolves lost their first three games, but then beat Philadelphia, 125–118, in overtime. They lost eight of their last nine games to finish at 22–60, yet averaged an NBA-record 26,160 fans per home game.

The following season they selected Louisville center Felton Spencer in the college draft with the sixth overall pick. Unlike the previous year, the Timberwolves finished strong, winning six of their last eight games to go 29–53. Things were looking up. Or were they? Musselman, and his entire coaching staff, was fired the day after the season ended. Jimmy Rodgers was named the new head coach.

The Timberwolves chose New Mexico center Luc Longley in the 1991 college draft with the seventh overall pick. Things didn't go well in 1991–92. Longley was a holdout for the first month of the season and Spencer was on and off the injured list. They finished 15–67. Jack McCloskey was brought in to head the basketball side of the front office, and he selected Dream Team player Christian Laettner with the third overall pick in the 1992 college draft. McCloskey then traded Richardson and Mitchell to the Indiana Pacers for Chuck Person and Micheal Williams. Things didn't improve. Rodgers was gone 29 games (6–23) into the season and was replaced by Lowe. The Timberwolves finished 19–63.

They improved to just 20–62 in 1993–94 and speculation swirled in Minnesota about whether or not the team would remain in Minneapolis or move to New Orleans, despite sellout crowds in The Target Center. The Wolves stayed, but won just 21 games under new coach Bill Blair. The Timberwolves were sold to Glen Taylor, a former U.S. Senator. He promoted former NBA great, and Minnesota native, Kevin McHale to V.P. of basketball operations. The Timberwolves used their first-round selection in the 1995 draft to obtain high school phenom Kevin Garnett. In 1995–96, Minnesota got off to a slow start and Blair was replaced on the sidelines by General Manager Phil "Flip" Saunders. At mid-season, Laettner was traded to Atlanta, and the Wolves finished 26–56.

McHale began tinkering with the roster; Saunders began feeling comfortable on the sidelines; Garnett began maturing as a player. The result? The Timberwolves wound up 40–42 in 1996–97 and qualified for the playoffs. They were swept in the first round by the Houston Rockets, but getting to post-season play for the first time was a step in the right direction for Minnesota.

In 1997–98, despite an injury that kept all-star Tom Gugliotta (20.1 points per game) on the sidelines for half the season, the Timberwolves finished 45–37. Garnett, also chosen to the all-star team, averaged 18.5 points and 9.6 rebounds a game. Stephon Marbury averaged 17.7 points and 8.6 assists per outing. In the playoffs, the Timberwolves extended the Seattle SuperSonics before losing the series, 3–2.

Copyright © 1998 Brian Spurlock/Spurlock Photography, Inc.

Kevin Garnett went straight from playing in high school to become a starter for the Wolves.

INDIVIDUAL RECORDS

Career

    Points: 6,216, Doug West, 1989–98

    Rebounds: 2,505, Sam Mitchell, 1989–92, 1995–98

    Assists: 1,973, Pooh Richardson, 1989–92

    Field Goal Pct.: .494, Kevin Garnett, 1995–98

    Free Throw Pct.: .877, Micheal Williams, 1992–98

Season

    Points: 1,903, Tony Campbell, 1989–90

    Rebounds: 708, Christian Laettner, 1992–93

    Assists: 734, Pooh Richardson, 1990–91

    Field Goal Pct.: .573, Dean Garrett, 1996–97

    Free Throw Pct.: .907, Micheal Williams, 1992–93

ACROSS

2. Fastbreak
5. A position
8. A cheer
10. Ricochet
15. Wheel tooth
16. ___-announcer (init.)
18. Players who try to score
19. Painted stripe
20. Whirlpool
21. West Coast rival (init.)
23. ___ or die
25. Extra period (abbr.)
27. Schedule of games
28. Named by *Newsweek* as 1 of the 100 most influential people for the next decade
29. Basket
31. Wolves' 1st round pick in '92 was a member of the Dream Team
33. Georgia Tech guard traded by Bucks on draft day in '96
36. 3-pointer in Rome
37. Rebound
39. Peruse a book
40. Fraction of a second
42. And so forth (abbr.)

43. Tip
44. Set NBA record with 97 consecutive FT made
46. Top of the body
48. ___ shoots, he scores!
49. Crafty
50. Louisville center traded to Utah in '93
51. Was ahead
52. Take the ball away
54. Make a basket
56. Team
58. Usual day part for game
59. Aussie center traded to Chicago in '94

DOWN

1. Carom at own basket (init.)
3. Home state of Tar Heels (init.)
4. Column heading on roster (abbr.)
5. Googs
6. Stadium
7. Triceps exercise
9. Type of shot
11. Blackman's nickname
12. VP/Basketball Operations and family
13. Passes leading to baskets
14. Point total at start of a game
17. At
22. Game sphere
23. Guard
24. Flip
26. Brad Lohaus' alma mater (init.)
29. Massage: back ___
30. Connecticut forward traded to Golden St. in '95
32. J.R.
33. Wolves' career rebounding leader
34. Wolves' career assists leader
35. ___ to guy
38. Everyone
41. Contests
44. Wolves' career scoring leader
45. Starting 5
47. Game
49. Capacity crowd (init.)
53. Away
55. Type of bread
56. ___-captain
57. TV talk: ___, Mom!

Solution on page 183

RETIRED UNIFORM NUMBERS

None

```
S  G  M  U  S  S  E  L  M  A  N  M  R  B  L
B  M  I  U  E  S  M  A  I  L  L  I  W  A  S
O  U  T  L  V  N  R  T  U  K  A  G  E  I  A
A  S  C  O  L  K  I  N  T  L  I  T  L  L  U
T  S  H  W  U  R  D  S  B  S  T  G  N  E  N
L  R  E  C  N  E  P  S  K  N  E  S  O  Y  D
L  M  L  A  R  L  B  H  E  O  N  W  S  R  E
A  A  L  M  O  R  R  R  S  E  O  S  D  O  R
H  R  M  P  O  I  N  M  E  E  S  R  R  S  S
S  B  L  B  D  K  I  W  R  U  R  E  A  R  I
R  U  E  E  S  T  X  L  O  L  E  Q  H  E  W
A  R  R  L  H  O  U  O  O  R  P  R  C  G  M
M  Y  C  L  A  R  D  S  O  W  B  I  I  D  R
G  A  R  N  E  T  T  R  E  R  E  T  R  O  P
M  T  A  T  T  O  I  L  G  U  G  L  L  R  C
```

BAILEY	LOWE	RIDER
BLAIR	MARBURY	RODGERS
BREUER	MARSHALL	ROOKS
BROWN	MITCHELL	SAUNDERS
CAMPBELL	MUSSELMAN	SMITH
GARNETT	PERSON	SPENCER
GUGLIOTTA	PORTER	WEST
LAETTNER	RICHARDSON	WILLIAMS

NEW JERSEY NETS

They say that if you stand at Times Square in Manhattan, you'll see everything eventually. Nets fans must feel as if their season tickets are located across the Hudson River at that Mecca of the civil and uncivilized world. They've surely seen a lot.

The New Jersey Nets began as the New Jersey Americans in the American Basketball Association in the summer of 1967. Coached by Max Zaslofsky and playing in the Teaneck Armory, their first team finished 36–43. That was good enough to tie for the final playoff spot with the Kentucky Colonels. A one-game tie-breaker was scheduled for New Jersey. The only problem was that a circus was already booked in the Armory. The game was scheduled for the Commack Arena on Long Island. But when the teams arrived, the floor was unplayable—uneven slats, nuts and bolts missing and out of place. The ABA commissioner ruled the game a forfeit and allowed Kentucky to advance into the playoffs.

The following summer the Americans were in need of a different home arena and settled on, of all places, Commack Arena. The Americans became the New York Nets. The team reached an all-time low with a mark of 17–61.

In 1969–70, Roy Boe purchased the team and moved it again, this time to Island Garden, at Hempstead, L.I. York Larese became the new coach and the Nets were able to lure Bill Melchionni from the Philadelphia 76ers. All of the changes paid off and the Nets went 39–45. Prior to the 1970–71 season, the Nets named Lou Carnesecca the head coach and acquired Rick Barry from the Virginia Squires. Barry averaged 29.4 points a game and led the Nets to a 40–44 record.

The Nets moved again, this time into the Nassau Veterans Memorial Coliseum in Uniondale, L.I., in the middle of the 1971–72 season. Barry averaged 31.5 points a game and the Nets finished 44–40. They beat Kentucky, 4 games to 2, and Virginia, 4–3, to win the Eastern Conference. But they lost to Indiana in the ABA Finals in six games.

Prior to the start of the 1972–73 season, the courts ordered Barry to return to the NBA. With him gone, the Nets fell to 30–54. But the Nets didn't stay down for long. They acquired Julius "Dr. J" Erving from Virginia and named Kevin Loughery coach. Dr. J averaged 27.4 points a game, and the Nets stormed to a 55–29 record and the ABA title. They won the championship series over Utah, 4–1.

The Nets continued their success by going 58–26 the following season, but lost in the first round of the playoffs to St. Louis, a team the Nets had swept, 12-zip in the regular season. In 1975–76, the final year of the ABA, the Nets won it all again. They went 55–29 and beat Denver in six games in the championship series. Dr. J averaged 29.3 points per game in the regular season and 34.6 in the playoffs in earning MVP honors. In the summer of 1976 the Nets moved again, this time from the ABA to the NBA. Erving was sold to Philadelphia before the start of the season, because of a contract dispute. The Nets finished 22–60 with Bubbles Hawkins leading the team with 19.3 points a game.

The franchise moved again (ho-hum), this time to the Rutgers Athletic Center in Piscataway, N.J., and became the New Jersey Nets. Bernard King had a spectacular rookie season, averaging 24.2 points and 9.5 rebounds a game, but the Nets finished 24–58. The team was sold to a partnership group headed by Joseph Taub and Alan Cohen in the summer of 1978 and the Nets qualified for their first NBA playoffs with a 37–45 record. But the Nets lost to Philadelphia in two straight games and were eliminated.

The next two seasons the Nets were out of the playoffs again, winning 34 and 24 games. Prior to the 1981–82 season, Larry Brown was named the head coach and the Nets moved once more, this time into the Brendon Byrne Arena in E. Rutherford, N.J. The Nets got off to a 3–12 start, but rebounded to wind up 44–38 and into the playoffs. The Nets played well again in 1982–83 and were headed for the playoffs when Brown resigned with six games remaining to take a job at the University of Kansas. The Nets were 47–29 at that point, but went 2–4 the rest of the way and were bounced out of the playoffs in two straight games.

That was the start of a slow and torturous decline. The Nets' victory total fell to 45, then 42, 39, 24, and 19. After a modest increase to 26 wins in 1988–89 under Coach Willis Reed, the Nets dropped again to 17 wins. The Nets improved to 26 victories in 1990–91 under Coach Bill Fitch, thanks to the play of newcomers Derrick Coleman, the No. 1 pick in the college draft, and Croatian Drazen Petrovic. The following year, the Nets improved to 40–42 and returned to the playoffs. Fitch resigned, but he was replaced by the U.S. Olympic coach, Chuck Daly. Daly guided the Nets to a 43–39 record, despite injuries to a number of key players. And the Nets received more bad news on June 7, 1993, when Petrovic was killed in an automobile accident in Germany.

The Nets still managed to finish 45–37 in 1993–94, but were eliminated in the first round of the playoffs by the New York Knicks. Daly had seen enough. He resigned following the season and was replaced by Butch Beard. The Nets fell to 30–52 the following season and with Coleman out for the start of the 1995–96 because of an injury, the disgruntled forward was dealt to Philadelphia for center Shawn Bradley. The Nets duplicated their 30–52 record. After the season, Beard was released and replaced by college coach John Calipari.

The rookie coach guided the Nets to a 26–56 mark in 1996–97. The Nets orchestrated an eight-player, draft-day trade that sent Keith Van Horn from the University of Utah to New Jersey. Van Horn was an instant success, leading the team in scoring with 19.7 points per game. The Nets finished 43–39 and qualified for the playoffs for the first time in four years.

Copyright © 1998 Brian Spurlock/Spurlock Photography, Inc.

Keith Van Horn led the Nets with 19.7 points per game as a rookie in 1997–98.

INDIVIDUAL RECORDS

Career

    Points: 10,440, Buck Williams, 1981–89

    Rebounds: 7,576, Buck Williams, 1981–89

    Assists: 2,363, Kenny Anderson, 1991–96

    Field Goal Pct.: .601, Darryl Dawkins, 1982–87

    Free Throw Pct.: .886, Mike Newlin, 1979–81

Season

    Points: 1,909, Bernard King, 1977–78

    Rebounds: 1,027, Buck Williams, 1982–83

    Assists: 801, Kevin Porter, 1977–78

    Field Goal Pct.: .644, Darryl Dawkins, 1985–86

    Free Throw Pct.: .893, Mike Gminski, 1985–86

ACROSS

1. A team color
3. Croatian killed in auto accident
6. Double team
9. Kendall Gill's alma mater (init.)
10. A division
13. Arena sign
14. Michael Ray
16. Kept on the scoreboard
18. Value of FG
20. Carom at own basket (init.)
21. ___ or die
24. Tear
26. 1st overall selection in '90 draft

28. 2nd in ABA scoring in 1970–71 and 1971–72
29. ___ shoots, he scores!
31. Away
32. ___ Green (init.)
33. Massage: back ___
34. Led Nets with 110 3-pointers in 1997–98
35. Spy
37. New Mexico St. star is Nets' career leader with 22.5 ppg
39. Hotels
40. Take the ball away (abbr.)
42. Rejection (init.)
43. Where severely injured players are sent (init.)

45. A cheer
47. Wager on a game
48. Make a basket
50. Team vehicles for trips from hotels to arenas
53. Lucious Harris' home state (abbr.)
54. Otis Birdsong's alma mater (init.)
57. Nets' head coach
60. Knicks, Celtics and 76ers
62. Column heading on roster (abbr.)
63. No game scheduled
65. Older player
66. Clear ___ to the basket
67. Contest
68. Throw

DOWN

2. Dribble hard to the basket
3. Tally
4. Go ___ guy
5. Rookie was leading scorer on 1997–98 team
6. Taps
7. Elbow or knee protection
8. Positions on the floor
11. Bill Jones' alma mater (init.)
12. Fall

13. Houston's Greg and Georgia Tech's Kenny
14. Blackman's nickname
15. Team physician (abbr.)
17. Type of x ray (init.)
19. Nets' career scoring leader
22. FGM divided by FGA
23. Logo registration (abbr.)
25. Nets' head coach, 1970–73
27. Milwaukee's Ray ___
30. Dr. J
31. Stomach muscle (abbr.)
32. Pass leading to a basket
36. Guard traded from K.C. for Cliff Robinson in '81
38. Not covered
41. Knots
44. Loud yell
46. Off the court (init.)
49. Fastbreak
51. Nets' head coach, 1992–94
52. Are victorious
55. TV talk: ___, Mom!
56. Squad
58. Position on the block
59. Treats a sprained ankle
61. Change direction sharply
64. Former
65. Against (abbr.)

Solution on page 184

RETIRED UNIFORM NUMBERS

3	Drazen Petrovic	25	Bill Melchionni
4	Wendall Ladner	32	Julius Erving
23	John Williamson		

```
G  S  O  R  E  N  C  Y  R  E  T  R  U  B  C
M  N  N  O  K  N  O  S  M  A  I  L  L  I  W
I  V  I  I  V  O  L  T  E  P  L  K  V  O  I
N  G  S  V  K  M  E  R  E  H  I  O  A  K  L
S  R  N  C  R  W  M  B  O  N  R  R  N  O  L
K  T  Y  I  D  E  A  W  G  T  A  Y  H  R  I
I  E  H  E  K  R  N  D  E  B  S  Y  O  E  A
I  P  E  K  R  R  W  P  O  R  T  E  R  N  M
R  R  N  Y  E  H  L  O  A  I  S  B  N  R  S
A  T  S  N  T  S  O  L  H  A  E  R  E  A  M
P  A  D  N  O  L  L  W  I  L  L  A  W  D  O
I  A  N  D  E  R  S  O  N  G  T  D  L  L  R
L  T  S  A  I  K  I  P  G  N  T  L  I  E  R
A  M  E  L  C  H  I  O  N  N  I  E  N  Y  I
C  Y  R  E  H  G  U  O  L  E  K  Y  I  N  S
```

ANDERSON	GMINSKI	O'KOREN
BARRY	KING	PETROVIC
BRADLEY	KITTLES	PORTER
CALIPARI	LADNER	REED
COLEMAN	LOUGHERY	VAN HORN
DAWKINS	MELCHIONNI	WILLIAMS
ERVING	MORRIS	WILLIAMSON
GILL	NEWLIN	WOHL

NEW YORK KNICKS

It was 1946 and the echoes of World War II still were ringing throughout the nation. The U.S. was looking for entertainment and sports were high on everyone's list. College basketball was popular in every major city, but professional teams were less than successful. On June 6, 1946, a group of men met at the Commodore Hotel in New York and changed the face of professional basketball.

Most of the men represented arenas from east coast cities that were making money on professional hockey. Among those in the group was Ned Irish, representing New York and the famed Madison Square Garden. "Count us in," said Irish. And the New York Knickerbockers were one of 11 teams in the first Basketball Association of America (later changed to the National Basketball Association).

There wasn't much time to get a team started, but Irish convinced former Manhattan College coach Neil Cohalan to oversee the task. Cohalan was able to round up a number of local college heroes, and the Knickerbockers opened the season Nov. 1 with a win in Toronto's famous Maple Leaf Gardens.

The Knickerbockers finished that first year at 33–27 and qualified for the playoffs. They made the playoffs in each of their first 10 seasons. Joe Lapchick was named the head coach after the inaugural season. He led the Knickerbockers to three consecutive NBA Finals from 1951–53. New York was beaten in all three, though, the first time by Rochester, the other two by the Minneapolis Lakers. From the mid-1950s to the mid-'60s, the Knicks (as they are now called) made the playoffs just once in 11 seasons. But the Knicks slowly had been acquiring talent. Part of the roster came from the draft: Willis Reed (1964), Bill Bradley (1965), Dave Stallworth (1965), Cazzie Russell (1966), Mike Riordan (1967) and Walt Frazier (1967). And part of the roster came from trades: Dick Barnett from the Los Angeles Lakers (1965) and Dave DeBusschere from the Detroit Pistons (1968).

New York got off to a 15–22 start in 1967–68 and Coach Dick McGuire was replaced by Red Holzman. The Knicks began winning almost immediately. The Knicks went 28–17 the rest of the way and qualified for the playoffs. Then they won a club-record 54 games the following year. Their expectations entering 1969–70 were the highest in a generation.

The Knicks responded by winning their first five games. They lost a game to San Francisco and then reeled off an NBA-record 18 consecutive victories (since broken) to go out of the gate at 23–1. They rolled to a 60–22 mark and an Eastern Division title. The Knicks struggled in the opening round of the playoffs, needing a double-overtime home-court victory in the first game and a home-court win in Game 7 to beat Baltimore. In the second round, the Knicks faced the Milwaukee Bucks with rookie center Lew Alcindor. The Knicks dispatched them, 4–1. That set up the NBA Finals against the Los Angeles Lakers. Wilt Chamberlain had missed all but the final month of the season for the Lakers, and Jerry West was coming off a 31.2 league-leading scoring average. It was a match-up of the two best teams from the two biggest cities. The first four games were split with each team going 1–1 at home. In Game 5 at New York, the Lakers built a big lead and appeared to be certain winners when Reed left the game with a knee injury. The Knicks outscored L.A., 32–18, in the fourth quarter to win, 107–100. With Reed on the sidelines, the Lakers coasted in Game 6, 135–113. But in Game 7, Reed hobbled onto the court and scored the game's first two baskets to ignite the crowd and his Knick teammates. Reed played only briefly, but New York won, 113–99, to claim the city's first NBA title.

The Knicks were bounced out of the Conference finals by Baltimore in 1971 and were beaten by the Lakers in the NBA Finals in 1972. The Knicks, who by then had added Earl "The Pearl" Monroe, Jerry Lucas and Phil Jackson to their roster, reached the Finals again in 1973. The foe was once more the L.A. Lakers. New York lost the opening game of the series in Los Angeles, then won four straight games to claim the title.

The Knicks' talent began to erode and the club slipped. They fell to 24 wins in 1984–85 and wound up with the No. 1 pick in the college draft. That selection turned out to be Patrick Ewing. The Knicks' fortunes didn't turn around overnight. They won just 23 games in 1985–86 and 24 in 1986–87, but Coach Rick Pitino led a brief surge with a division title in 1988–89. Pitino departed and after a two-year lag, Pat Riley was hired as coach to revive the Knicks. New York won 51 games in 1991–92 and had the best record in the Eastern Conference in 1992–93 with 60 victories. But the Knicks lost in the playoffs both seasons to the eventual champion Chicago Bulls.

They continued their progress in 1993–94. The Knicks wound up 57–25, and advanced to within one victory of the NBA championship. They beat New Jersey, Chicago and Indiana in the playoffs before facing the Houston Rockets in the Finals. The Knicks were ahead, 3 games to 2, before losing the final two games in Houston.

New York won 55 games in 1994–95, but after being beaten by Indiana in the second round of the playoffs, Riley parted company on less than friendly terms. Veteran Don Nelson was summoned to pick up the pieces, but he called it quits midway through the season. Assistant Coach Jeff Van Gundy succeeded him and led the Knicks to a 47–35 record. New York upset Cleveland, 3–0, in the first round of the playoffs, then succumbed to the eventual champions, the Chicago Bulls, 4–1, in the second round.

The Knicks finished 57–25 in 1996–97, but were bounced out of the second round of the playoffs, then were 43–39 in 1997–98. Ewing missed 56 games with a wrist injury. The Knicks upset Miami (coached by Riley) in the opening round of the playoffs, but lost to the Pacers in Round Two.

Copyright © 1996 Brian Spurlock/Spurlock Photography, Inc.

Patrick Ewing holds the NBA Finals record of 8 blocked shots in a game.

INDIVIDUAL RECORDS

Career

Points: 22,079, Patrick Ewing, 1985–98

Rebounds: 9,778, Patrick Ewing, 1985–98

Assists: 4,791, Walt Frazier, 1967–77

Field Goal Pct.: .552, Bill Cartwright, 1979–88

Free Throw Pct.: .886, Kiki Vandeweghe, 1988–92

Season

Points: 2,347, Patrick Ewing, 1989–90

Rebounds: 1,191, Willis Reed, 1968–69

Assists: 868, Mark Jackson, 1987–88

Field Goal Pct.: .572, Bernard King, 1983–84

Free Throw Pct.: .899, Kiki Vandeweghe, 1990–91

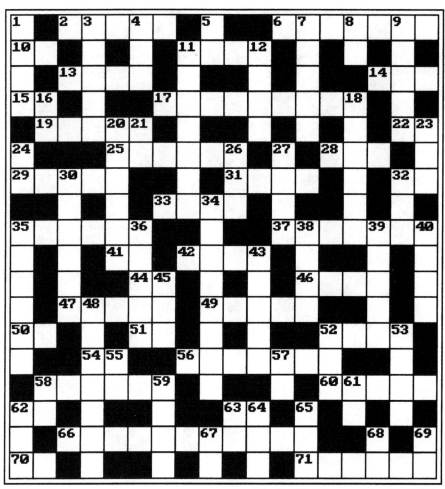

ACROSS

2. Ricochet
6. Clyde
10. Former
11. Swats
13. Defeat
14. Are victorious
15. ___ or die
17. Knicks' Jeff and Heat's Stan
19. Squads
22. A cheer
25. Power forward traded to Toronto in '98
28. Trick defense: ___-and-1

29. Set Knicks record with 3,457 minutes in 1995–96
31. Makes mistakes
32. Players get 6 a game (init.)
33. Days off with games
35. His 26.9 ppg in 1978–79 is 4th best by a Knick
37. NBA Finals foe in '94
41. Where severely injured players are sent (init.)
42. Officials (abbr.)
44. A cheer
46. Knicks' conference
47. Team
49. Former mode of team travel

50. Carom at own basket (init.)
51. Phil Jackson's native state (init.)
52. 30-and-___ league
54. Stomach muscle (abbr.)
56. Official spokesman for NBA Authentics merchandise
58. Quarter
60. Arm joint
62. Away
63. Off the court (init.)
66. All-star forward also was major league pitcher
70. Logo registration (abbr.)
71. Ducat

DOWN

1. Ahead
3. Stadium
4. In and ___
5. ___-announcer (init.)
7. Captain of '73 championship team and family
8. Mourning's nickname
9. Knicks' career scoring leader
11. Power forward turned senator
12. Partial ticket
16. Extra period (abbr.)
18. Bottom half of a uniform
20. Earl the Pearl
21. Texas rival (init.)
23. Points ___ turnovers
24. Cazzie Russell's alma mater (init.)

26. Marv Albert's call
27. Shape of path of long jump shot
30. Partner in Original Man Wear clothing company
32. Paid player
34. Thrown out of the game by an official
35. Coach
36. Arena music maker
38. Not covered
39. Championship
40. Cross-town rivals
43. Discolored spot
45. Weird
48. Period
52. Point value of FT
53. Nickname for 1st year player
55. Can go both ways
57. Take away the ball (abbr.)
58. Tally (abbr.)
59. Slang for assist
61. West Coast rival (init.)
62. Try (abbr.)
63. 1st word of the national anthem
64. Wager on a game
65. Type of shot
67. ___-captain
68. Kenny Walker's alma mater (init.)
69. 1-pointer

Solution on page 184

RETIRED UNIFORM NUMBERS

10	Walt Frazier	19	Willis Reed
12	Dick Barnett	22	Dave DeBusschere
15	Earl Monroe	24	Bill Bradley
15	Dick McGuire	613	Red Holzman

```
P  G  B  A  R  N  E  T  T  L  H  K  D  I  G
R  M  S  I  S  H  Y  D  N  O  G  C  E  V  C
T  O  M  E  L  O  G  G  L  C  G  I  B  C  A
O  N  A  K  L  G  Y  Z  N  U  L  H  U  H  R
Y  R  I  R  U  U  M  E  E  I  A  C  S  H  T
O  O  L  M  A  A  S  R  L  L  K  P  S  E  W
N  E  L  N  N  Y  I  R  N  I  N  A  C  B  R
O  L  I  U  E  N  S  R  E  I  R  L  H  R  I
S  W  W  L  G  K  N  B  E  E  N  E  E  A  G
N  E  K  I  R  O  R  O  R  I  D  R  R  D  H
H  A  I  A  S  A  L  O  G  D  U  I  E  L  T
O  I  T  K  U  L  Z  A  N  N  N  U  E  E  S
J  S  C  N  P  C  H  N  I  T  A  G  L  Y  G
V  A  N  G  U  N  D  Y  W  J  O  C  R  E  N
J  R  E  I  Z  A  R  F  E  N  R  M  B  A  N
```

BARNETT	GREEN	MONROE
BRADLEY	GUERIN	NAULLS
BRAUN	HOLZMAN	OAKLEY
CARTWRIGHT	JACKSON	REED
DEBUSSCHERE	JOHNSON	RILEY
EWING	KING	STARKS
FRAZIER	LAPCHICK	VAN GUNDY
GOLA	MCGUIRE	WILLIAMS

ORLANDO MAGIC

Do you believe in luck? In Orlando, there's no such thing as luck, just Magic. And it was that Blue, Silver and Black Magic that allowed Orlando to defy the odds and wind up with the No. 1 pick in the college draft two years in a row. The Magic parlayed those selections into Shaquille O'Neal, Anfernee Hardaway and three more future first-round draft picks.

Orlando's entry into the NBA required a bit of magic itself. In September, 1985, Jim Hewitt, an Orlando businessman, convinced Philadelphia 76ers General Manager Pat Williams to join him in trying to get an NBA team for the Disney World area. Hewitt found 31 other investors to come up with the necessary capital to pay the $32.5 million expansion fee and other start-up costs. In January, 1987, Hewitt and Williams met with the expansion committee in New York and three months later a franchise was awarded. The Magic began play in the 1989–90 season. Matt Goukas was hired as the head coach in the spring of 1988 and Bob Weiss was named his assistant. On June 15, 1989, Orlando took part in the expansion draft of veteran NBA players. The Magic chose 12 players: Sidney Green, Reggie Theus, Terry Catledge, Sam Vincent, Otis Smith, Scott Skiles, Jerry Reynolds, Mark Acres, Morlon Wiley, Jim Farmer, Keith Lee and Frank Johnson. Two weeks later the Magic selected Illinois' Nick Anderson with the 11th pick in the college draft. Of those 13 players, 10 made the opening-day roster.

The Magic dropped their first game on Nov. 4, 1989, to New Jersey, 111–106, but won their second and third games over New York and Cleveland. The Magic surprised everyone by going 7–7 in their first month. Things deteriorated in a hurry. The Magic went 2–13 in December and lost 24 of their final 26 games to finish 18–64. The Magic selected Georgia Tech's Dennis Scott with the fourth overall pick in the 1990 college draft, and Greg Kite was signed as a free agent. The Magic became the best of the four most recent expansion teams by winning 31 games in 1990–91.

Prior to the 1991–92 season, the Magic was sold to Rich DeVos, co-founder and president of the Amway Corporation. They added Arizona's Brian Williams through the draft. Williams was a hold-out, then was hurt. Injuries played a big part in the Magic losing 17 straight games on their way to a 21–61 mark.

By virtue of having the second worst record in the league, the Magic received 10 (out of the total of 66) Ping-Pong balls in the hopper for the weighted draft lottery on May 17, 1992. Despite the odds, the Magic wound up with the No. 1 selection. That pick turned out to be LSU's 7-foot-1, 300-pound Shaquille O'Neal. O'Neal didn't disappoint the scouts or the fans. He was an immediate success on the floor and off. He averaged 23.4 points, 13.9 rebounds and 3.53 blocked shots a game, while shooting 56.2 percent from the field. He also became one of the most popular players in the game for fans and advertising agencies.

With O'Neal, an all-star and Rookie of the Year, the Magic improved to 41–41. They tied the Indiana Pacers for eighth place in the Eastern Conference and the final playoff spot. The first tie-breaker is results of games against each other. The teams split their four games in the regular season. The second tie-breaker is better winning percentage within their own conference. Both teams were 27–29. The third tie-breaker is better winning percentage within their own division, but only if the tied teams are in the same division. Since the Magic and Pacers are in different divisions, that tie-breaker didn't apply. The fourth tie-breaker is better winning percentage against playoff opponents in their own conference. Again, the two teams had identical marks. The fifth tie-breaker is point differential in games against each other. The Magic led in the first game by 20 points in the final period. They rested their regulars and saw their margin of victory slip to 14. The Pacers won Game 2 by 16. Orlando won Game 3 by 13, and the Pacers won the final game of the series by 16 points. Tie-breaker: Pacers with a +5. The margin at the time seemed meaningless. But in this case, it made the difference between the Magic participating in the franchise's first playoffs or staying at home. Williams and Magic fans cried foul, but after Lottery Day the complaining stopped.

Because Orlando had the best record of any of the lottery participants, they had just one Ping-Pong ball in the hopper. Its chances of getting the No. 1 pick were 65-to-1. But Magic prevailed once again and Orlando had the No. 1 pick in the 1993 college draft. It used the pick to select Michigan's Chris Webber, but by a pre-arranged agreement, Orlando swapped Webber to Golden State which had selected Memphis State's Hardaway with the third pick. Golden State also sweetened the pot with three additional first-round picks in future drafts.

Goukas resigned as coach the day before the draft, and he was replaced by assistant Brian Hill. O'Neal and Hardaway didn't disappoint too many of their fans in the 1993–94 season. Orlando went 50–32 and qualified for the playoffs for the first time. O'Neal finished second in the NBA in scoring (29.3 points per game), second in rebounding (13.2 per game), first in field goal percentage (.599) and sixth in blocked shots (2.85 per game). Yet, the Magic were upset in their first playoff series by the Indiana Pacers, 3–0.

The early departure from the playoffs inspired the Magic in 1994–95. Orlando rolled to a 57–25 record in winning the Atlantic Division and recorded the best record in the Eastern Conference. The Magic beat Boston and Chicago in the playoffs to set up a rematch with the Pacers, this time for the Conference championship. The Magic used the home court advantage to win the series, 4–3. But Orlando ran into the Houston Rockets in the NBA Finals and lost, 4–0.

The Magic repeated as Division champions in 1995–96 and finished 60–22. O'Neal (26.6 ppg) and Hardaway (21.7 ppg) provided one of the league's best 1–2 combos. The Magic beat Detroit and Atlanta in the playoffs before losing to Chicago, 4–0, in the Conference finals.

That's when the Magic's lucky horseshoe began to turn upside down. O'Neal departed Orlando for starry Los Angeles. When the Magic got off to a 24–25 start in 1996–97, Hill was out as head coach after a vote of the players. Richie Adubato closed out the season as head coach. The Magic finished 45–37 and were eliminated in the first round of the playoffs.

Chuck Daly, a two-time NBA championship head coach at Detroit, was hired to lead the Magic in 1997–98. Hardaway suffered through injuries and was limited to 19 games. Only one player on the roster was able to play in all 82 games. Orlando was 41–41 and failed to make the playoffs for the first time in five years.

Penny Hardaway was a member of the 1996 U.S. Olympic team.

INDIVIDUAL RECORDS

Career

Points: 9,949, Nick Anderson, 1988–98

Rebounds: 3,691, Shaquille O'Neal, 1992–96

Assists: 2,776, Scott Skiles, 1989–94

Field Goal Pct.: .581, Shaquille O'Neal, 1992–96

Free Throw Pct.: .892, Scott Skiles, 1989–94

Season

Points: 2,377, Shaquille O'Neal, 1993–94

Rebounds: 1,122, Shaquille O'Neal, 1992–93

Assists: 735, Scott Skiles, 1992–93

Field Goal Pct.: .599, Shaquille O'Neal, 1993–94

Free Throw Pct.: .902, Scott Skiles, 1990–91

ACROSS

1. Easy shot
4. Magic's 1st head coach
8. Nick Anderson's alma mater (init.)
10. Backboard
11. Texas rival (init.)
13. Penny and Lil' Penny
17. Former home of the Hawks: ___ Louis
18. Up and ___
19. Yells
21. Intercept passes
23. Set NBA record with 30 assists in '90 game

24. Full court pressure
29. Magic's head coach, 1993–97
30. Skiles and Dennis
31. Fruit drink
32. Deadlock
33. Simple
34. Slogan for protesters of shoe maker (2 words)
36. Team's best player
37. Participant
39. West Coast rival (init.)
41. Breakfast food
43. Game sphere
45. Expected time of touchdown (init.)

46. Official's decision
49. Top half of a uniform
51. ___ shoots, he scores!
52. Extra FT
54. ___-announcer (init.)
55. Monetary penalty
57. Throw
61. Tally (abbr.)
62. After lay or warm
63. Dream Team: Team ___
64. Can't tell the players without a ___.

DOWN

2. Arena sign
3. Qtr.
4. Horace and Harvey
5. Top of the ___
6. Back court scorer (pos.)
7. Playing years
8. ___ vs. Them
9. Pass leading to a basket
12. Away
13. TV talk: ___, Mom!
14. Magic's career scoring leader
15. Get back to me quickly (init.)
16. Against (abbr.)

20. Michigan St. guard traded to Milwaukee for Lester Conner
22. Greek center acquired from Golden St.
24. Participate
25. Throw out of the game
26. Slate of games
27. 1st year player
28. Try a 1-pointer (init.)
32. Championship
35. Roster spot for hurt players (init.)
37. Postseason
38. 3-pt. line
40. Try
42. Night before a game
44. Stadium
47. Capable
48. Alley-oops
49. Dunks
50. Magic's career scoring leader
53. Jam
56. Column heading on roster (abbr.)
58. Todd Lichti's alma mater (init.)
59. Publicity (init.)
60. Derek Harper's position (init.)

Solution on page 185

RETIRED UNIFORM NUMBERS

None

```
C  O  B  L  A  E  N  O  W  R  E  H  G  R  D
T  K  N  O  B  M  A  R  O  M  T  R  T  E  K
U  O  W  E  W  I  E  Y  L  I  E  L  S  Y  I
R  T  S  I  A  I  A  Y  M  E  R  U  M  N  S
N  I  H  C  N  L  E  S  N  N  E  E  R  O  M
E  E  A  O  O  W  S  N  N  H  D  E  U  L  I
R  E  R  I  A  T  C  E  T  A  T  G  E  D  T
T  N  D  D  E  E  T  O  S  N  V  D  H  S  S
S  O  A  S  N  I  O  N  E  S  C  E  T  T  H
E  S  W  E  K  N  Y  C  A  S  K  L  O  K  A
H  R  A  I  S  A  N  L  T  R  H  T  L  J  W
O  E  Y  K  O  I  C  R  A  D  G  A  L  I  O
T  D  R  A  V  R  O  N  G  D  F  C  A  E  H
I  N  N  L  L  N  Y  E  O  S  E  L  I  K  S
C  A  T  Y  G  D  G  U  O  K  A  S  A  S  I
```

ANDERSON	HARDAWAY	SEIKALY
BOWIE	HILL	SHAW
CATLEDGE	KITE	SKILES
DALY	KONCAK	SMITH
EVANS	O'NEAL	STRONG
GRANT	REYNOLDS	THEUS
GREEN	ROYAL	TURNER
GUOKAS	SCOTT	VINCENT

PHILADELPHIA 76ERS

Maybe the greatest team and maybe the worst team. The Philadelphia 76ers can offer up pretty good arguments for both. And amazingly, they came only six years apart.

The 1966–67 Sixers compiled a record of 68–13. They were 37–3 at one point and 46–4 at another. In the playoffs, they cruised past the Cincinnati Royals and Oscar Robertson, 3 games to 1, blitzed the Bill Russell-led Boston Celtics, 4–1, and then in the championship series, beat Rick Barry and his San Francisco Warriors, 4–2.

Wilt Chamberlain was the leader of the Sixers and the most dominating player in the league at the time. He averaged 24.1 points a game (3rd in the league), 24.2 rebounds (1st in the league), 7.8 assists (3rd in the league) and shot .683 from the field (1st in the league). But Philadelphia was also one of the most balanced teams in history.

The guards were Hal Greer (22.1 points and 3.8 assists per game), Larry Costello (7.8 points and 2.9 assists) and Wally Jones (13.2 points and 3.7 assists). The forwards were Billy Cunningham (18.5 points and 7.3 rebounds), Chet Walker (19.3 points and 8.1 rebounds) and Lucious Jackson (12.0 points and 8.9 rebounds). Also coming off the bench were Dave Gambee, Bill Melchionni, Matt Goukas and Bob Weiss. The team was coached by Alex Hannum.

Six years later, the 1972–73 Sixers finished 9–73. They were 0–15 at one point and 4–58 at another. They also lost their final 13 games and finished 59 games behind first-place Boston. A total of 19 players saw action for Philadelphia. The leading scorer was Fred Carter with 20.0 points a game. Greer was the only player on both teams. He averaged 5.6 points, then retired at the end of the season. The team was coached by Roy Rubin (4–47) and Kevin Loughery (5–26).

Even before those two teams, the Sixers had their ups and downs. The franchise began in 1949–50 as the Syracuse Nationals who merged into the NBA from the National Basketball League. Al Cervi was a player/coach for the first seven-and-a-half years. He guided the Nationals to a 51–13 record and first place in the Eastern Division in their first season. They lost to the Minneapolis Lakers in the NBA Finals, 4–2. The Nationals returned to the Finals in 1953–54 and lost to the Lakers again. But in 1954–55 they won the title over Ft. Wayne, 4–3. Dolph Schayes led the Nats with 18.5 points a game.

Syracuse was around .500 for the next decade until it moved to Philadelphia in the summer of 1963 and became the "76ers." Schayes took over as the head coach. The 76ers were 34–46 in their first season and improved to 40–40 in 1964–65. Midway through that season the 76ers acquired Chamberlain. Philadelphia had to part with Paul Neumann, Connie Dierking, Lee Shaffer and cash to get Chamberlain back to his hometown. The 76ers had the best record in the league in 1965–66 at 55–25, but they were bounced out of the playoffs in the Division finals by Boston, 4–1. Hannum was brought in to coach the following season, the Sixers' best ever.

They went 62–20 in 1967–68 and Chamberlain was traded to the Lakers, July 9, 1968. Jack Ramsay took over as coach, and the Sixers slipped to 55 wins, then 42. They rebounded to 47 wins in 1970–71, but fell to 30 the next season. Ramsay departed, and Rubin entered for the infamous season of doom.

After the fiasco of 1972–73, Gene Shue was named the head coach, and the team improved for five straight seasons. After a 50-win season in 1976–77, the Sixers advanced to the NBA Finals, but lost to the Portland Trail Blazers, 4–2.

Cunningham took over the coaching reins midway through the 1977–78 season and the Sixers continued their rise. They won 59 games in 1979–80 and made it to the Finals again, this time losing to the Lakers, 4–2. Two years later, they were in the Finals once more, but lost again to the Lakers, 4–2.

The stars for the Sixers during that period were Julius "Dr. J" Erving, Bobby Jones, Darryl Dawkins and Doug Collins. Dawkins was known for shattering two backboards in a 22-day period in 1979, leading to the creation of collapsible rims.

Injuries and old age caught up with Philly, and despite the emergence of all-star Charles Barkley, the Sixers experienced a decline (by their standards) through the rest of the 1980s. They won 53 games in 1989–90, but followed that with 44 and 35.

Prior to the 1992–93 season, Barkley was traded to Phoenix, and the Sixers fell to 26–56 and out of the playoffs for the second straight season.

In the 1993 college draft, Philadelphia picked 7-foot-6 Shawn Bradley from BYU with the second overall selection. Paired with 7-foot-7 Manute Bol, the Sixers had the two tallest players in league history. But Bol soon was gone and Bradley failed to reach the lofty expectations (and was eventually traded to New Jersey for Derrick Coleman). In the 1993–94 season, Fred Carter's first full season as head coach, the Sixers slid to 25–57. He was replaced in the summer of 1994 by an enthusiastic John Lucas.

The Sixers suffered through 24- and 18-win campaigns. A total of 24 different players donned Philly's red jerseys in 1995–96, to no avail. Following the season, Lucas was replaced by Johnny Davis. Davis' tenure lasted just one season after the Sixers finished 22–60, despite having the NBA Rookie of the Year, Allen Iverson. Enter Larry Brown, the master of turning around under-performing teams.

Not even Brown could retool the team fast enough. He used 22 different players en route to a 31–51 record. He then used the eighth pick in the draft to select St. Louis guard Larry Hughes.

Allen Iverson was the NBA Rookie of the Year in 1997.

Copyright © 1998 Brian Spurlock/Spurlock Photography, Inc.

INDIVIDUAL RECORDS

Career

Points: 21,586, Hal Greer, 1963–73

Rebounds: 11,256, Dolph Schayes, 1948–64

Assists: 6,212, Maurice Cheeks, 1978–89

Field Goal Pct.: .583, Wilt Chamberlain, 1964–68

Free Throw Pct.: .881, Scott Brooks, 1988–90

Season

Points: 2,649, Wilt Chamberlain, 1965–66

Rebounds: 1,957, Wilt Chamberlain, 1966–67

Assists: 753, Maurice Cheeks, 1985–86

Field Goal Pct.: .683, Wilt Chamberlain, 1966–67

Free Throw Pct.: .938, Mike Gminski, 1987–88

ACROSS

1. Road ___
3. Teams
6. Taps
10. Tim McCormick's alma mater (init.)
11. D.C.
12. Sir Charles
16. Against (abbr.)
18. Side position on the court
20. Column heading on roster (abbr.)
21. North Carolina swingman traded to Pistons in '98
23. To the inside
25. Move up
26. Make defensive stands
28. Jump shooting free thrower
32. Away
33. Move smoothly
34. ___ the line
37. TV talk: ___, Mom!
38. Blackman's nickname
39. Sixers' head coach
41. Center acquired from Houston for Caldwell Jones and a No. 1 pick
45. Basket
47. Contest
48. West Coast rival (init.)

49. Leap
51. Carom at own basket (init.)
52. Nickname for 1st year player
53. Painted stripe
54. Fastener on warm-up pants
56. Former
59. Super agent: ___ Tellem
60. Leg joint
62. Basket interference
66. Go ___ guy
67. Ref's hand gesture

DOWN

1. Moses Malone's uniform number
2. NBA Rookie of the Year in 1996–97
4. Joe Bryant's alma mater (init.)
5. Defeat
6. Deadlock
7. Day for NBC games (abbr.)
8. Ohio St. swingman has a pet eel
9. Rex Walters' alma mater (init.)
11. All-star forward was head coach from 1977–85
13. Easy shot
14. Whirlpool
15. Mike Price's alma mater (init.)
17. Sixers' career field goal pct. leader
18. 1st player at Southern Miss. to have his uniform number retired
19. Larry Costello's alma mater (init.)
22. Illinois St. guard was the 1st overall pick in the '73 draft
23. Treats a sprained ankle
24. Pass leading to a basket (abbr.)
27. ___-announcer (init.)
29. Destroy
30. Mike Dunleavy's alma mater (init.)
31. Tally (abbr.)
35. Off the court (init.)
36. ___ or die
37. Basket
40. All-star guard traded to Chicago for Jim Washington in '69
42. Isaac Austin's alma mater (init.)
43. Dr. J
44. ___ shoots, he scores!
46. Larry Brown's running mate in college, he also became an NBA head coach
49. Athletic supporter
50. Play ___ or trade me!
55. Protection for knees and elbows
57. Basket cord
58. Mode of team transportation
61. South Bend university (init.)
63. Extra period (abbr.)
64. Where severely injured players are sent (init.)
65. Up and ___

Solution on page 185

RETIRED UNIFORM NUMBERS

6	Julius Erving	15	Hal Greer
10	Maurice Cheeks	24	Bobby Jones
13	Wilt Chamberlain	32	Billy Cunningham

```
O   B   A   R   K   L   E   Y   I   C   E   R   V   I   M
C   U   R   A   R   E   S   U   O   H   K   C   A   T   S
N   D   S   A   I   R   R   R   A   E   K   O   O   R   C
O   Y   N   E   D   S   E   V   R   W   L   S   I   A   H
O   M   I   K   U   L   V   E   I   E   S   T   E   M   A
P   A   A   O   F   H   E   E   R   N   K   E   R   S   Y
S   H   L   A   F   N   S   Y   S   G   G   L   S   A   E
R   G   R   B   A   K   G   M   N   E   B   L   O   Y   S
E   N   E   E   R   G   C   S   I   O   N   O   L   E   A
H   I   B   S   S   O   K   O   L   X   L   O   L   N   V
T   M   M   A   A   E   W   E   L   C   U   A   J   O   I
A   N   A   T   E   E   N   N   O   B   K   O   M   L   S
E   U   H   H   K   A   H   S   C   O   L   E   M   A   N
W   C   C   U   N   N   I   N   G   H   A   M   O   M   H
C   X   N   O   S   R   E   V   I   A   H   C   S   N   C
```

BARKLEY	COLEMAN	KERR
BLOCK	COLLINS	MALONE
BOL	COSTELLO	MIX
BRADLEY	CUNNINGHAM	RAMSAY
BROWN	ERVING	SCHAYES
CERVI	GREER	SHUE
CHAMBERLAIN	IVERSON	STACKHOUSE
CHEEKS	JONES	WEATHERSPOON

PHOENIX SUNS

Jerry Colangelo was named the Suns' first general manager on Mar. 1, 1968. Then 28, Colangelo was the youngest general manager in professional sports. Today, he is part-owner, president and chief executive officer of the team. In between, Colangelo had two stints as an interim coach, oversaw the building of America West Arena, won several distinguished service awards and probably swept a floor or two. Today, he also oversees the operation of Major League Baseball's Arizona Diamondbacks.

In his tenure with the Suns he's seen a few ups and downs. The first up was seeing Phoenix get a franchise and the work it took to get the first team on the floor for the 1968–69 season. Johnny "Red" Kerr was named the first coach. The first college player drafted was Gary Gregor, a 6-foot-7 forward from South Carolina. The first player selected in the expansion draft was Dick Van Arsdale. But euphoria turned to sorrow as the Suns lost their final seven games to go a league-worst 16–66.

By all rights, the Suns should have had the No. 1 selection in the 1969 college draft, but three years earlier the NBA instituted a coin-flip between the last-place teams in each division to keep clubs from being tempted to lose games intentionally. So, Phoenix was involved with Milwaukee in a coin-toss for the No. 1 pick. The Suns called heads. The coin came up tails. Milwaukee drafted Lew Alcindor. The Suns picked Neal Walk.

That summer the Suns also picked up veterans Paul Silas and Connie Hawkins and improved to 39–43. Kerr resigned 38 games into the season, and he was replaced by Colangelo. The Suns won their final four games to qualify for their first ever playoffs. In the first round the Suns faced the Los Angeles Lakers, featuring Wilt Chamberlain, Jerry West and Elgin Baylor. The Lakers won the first game, but the Suns then won three games in a row to take a commanding lead. The Lakers regrouped and won the series, 4 games to 3, en route to advancing all the way to the NBA Finals. Even though the Suns lost the series, they captured the hearts of the city and the rest of the NBA.

By 1970–71 Van Arsdale was the only original Sun remaining. Off-season trades brought Mel Counts and Clem Haskins to Phoenix, and Cotton Fitzsimmons was named the new coach. The Suns rolled to a 48–34 record, yet failed to make the playoffs.

In 1971–72, the Suns picked up Charlie Scott at mid-season and improved to 49–33, but again, failed to qualify for the playoffs. Bill van Breda Kolff was hired as coach in the summer of 1972, but he was fired seven games into the season. Colangelo took over on the bench again. The Suns stumbled to a 38–44 mark.

John MacLeod was named the head coach prior to the 1973–74 season, and after a couple of shaky years, the Suns enjoyed their most exciting season ever. It was 1975–76. Phoenix acquired Paul Westphal in an off-season trade and drafted center Alvan Adams and guard Ricky Sobers. The Suns were 18–27 at the all-star break and appeared headed for nowhere. But they traded for Gar Heard, caught on fire and went 24–13 the rest of the way to finish at 42–40. Phoenix did make the playoffs and eliminated Seattle in the Conference semifinals, 4–2. They then beat the defending champion Golden State Warriors, 4–3, to advance to the NBA Finals. In the Finals the Suns faced the Boston Celtics. Boston eventually prevailed, 4–2, but Game 5 went down in history as the greatest playoff game ever. It took Boston three excruciating overtimes to beat Phoenix, 128–126.

Injuries knocked out the Suns' entire front line in 1976–77, and they fell to 34–48. Phoenix rebounded to 49–33 the following season, then began a run of three straight 50+ win seasons. Westphal was scoring more than 20 points a game, as was Walter Davis. The Suns capped the run with a 57–25 mark in 1980–81 and their first division title, but were unable to return to the NBA Finals.

The Suns slipped to 46 wins in 1981–82, but got back over the 50-win mark in 1982–83 at 53–29. The Suns wish their fans would forget those next five years. The victory totals slid from 41 to 36 to 32 to 36 to 28. There was a well-publicized drug scandal that rocked the franchise and the NBA. The team received a complete overhaul.

The new faces included Tom Chambers, Kevin Johnson, Mark West and Dan Majerle. Fitzsimmons returned as the head coach. The Suns returned to prominence with three consecutive 50-win seasons. Not satisfied with standing pat after a 53–29 record in 1991–92, Colangelo dealt three players to Philadelphia for all-star Charles Barkley.

Barkley didn't waste any time showing his worth. He averaged 25.6 points and 12.2 rebounds a game in leading Phoenix to a league-best 62–20 mark. He was the consensus league MVP. The Suns, under the direction of rookie coach Westphal, advanced to the NBA Finals before losing to the Chicago Bulls, 4–2.

Then in 1993–94, with Barkley nursing a sore back, the Suns slid to 56–26 and were eliminated in the second round of the playoffs. The Suns won their division again in 1994–95, but were stunned in the second round of the playoffs again. When they got off to a worse than expected start in 1995–96, Westphal was replaced by—who else?—Fitzsimmons. The Suns finished 41–41, but were bounced out of the first round of the playoffs.

When the Suns got off to an 0–8 start under Fitzsimmons in 1996–97, he was replaced by Danny Ainge. Phoenix went 40–34 the rest of the way and qualified for the playoffs. The following year, the Suns finished 56–26. Rex Chapman (15.9 points per game) led a balanced scoring attack that featured six players in double-figures. However, the Suns were upset in the first round of the playoffs by San Antonio, 3 games to 1.

Copyright © 1998 Brian Spurlock/Spurlock Photography, Inc.

Antonio McDyess led the Suns in points and rebounds in 1997–98.

INDIVIDUAL RECORDS
Career

  Points: 15,666, Walter Davis, 1977–88

  Rebounds: 6,937, Alvan Adams, 1975–88

  Assists: 5,841, Kevin Johnson, 1988–98

  Field Goal Pct.: .614, Mark West, 1987–94

  Free Throw Pct.: .884, Kyle Macy, 1980–85

Season

  Points: 2,201, Tom Chambers, 1989–90

  Rebounds: 1,015, Paul Silas, 1970–71

  Assists: 991, Kevin Johnson, 1988–89

  Field Goal Pct.: .653, Mark West, 1988–89

  Free Throw Pct.: .917, Eddie Johnson, 1989–90

ACROSS

1. Slate of games
6. Hoop
10. Suns' career FT pct. leader
11. Metal basket
12. Suns' career assists leader
15. Usual mode of team travel
16. Forward has a restaurant/bar near arena
18. West Coast rival (init.)
19. Chewed by some players
23. Suns' career rebounding leader
24. ORU's Alvin or UNC's Charlie
27. Fitzsimmons
29. ___ or die

30. Position on the block
32. Super agent: ___ Tellem
33. Equipment mgr.'s activity
34. Finish
35. Part of a sneaker
36. Vicinity
38. Part owner, CEO of Suns/Coyotes/Diamondbacks
41. Deadlocks
42. Kept on the scoreboard (abbr.)
43. Fan's beverage
45. Suns' 1st head coach
46. Toss
48. Part of FGA
49. Neither's partner

50. Paul Westphal's alma mater (init.)
52. 3-pt. line
54. Arm joint
56. No game scheduled today
57. Foot covers
60. Logo registration (abbr.)
63. Player who begins a game
65. Jerseys and shorts
66. Column heading on roster (abbr.)

DOWN

2. Official's decision
3. Barkley and Johnson: Dynamic ___
4. The paint
5. Hoosier twins Tom and Dick
6. Play-___-play announcer
7. Take the ball away (abbr.)
8. Where severely injured players are sent (init.)
9. Championship
10. TV talk: Hi, ___!
13. Team physician (abbr.)
14. Suns' all-star turned head coach
15. 1-pointer (init.)
17. Nealy and Pinckney

19. Official to heckler: ___ life! (2 words)
20. All-star forward's father was pro player, too
21. Suns' career scoring leader
22. 1988–89 NBA 6th Man of the Year
25. Signed with Suns in '88 as the 1st unrestricted free agent in NBA history
26. Throw the ball away (abbr.)
28. Carom at own basket (init.)
31. Players' shoes
37. Sir Charles was league MVP in 1992–93
39. Miscues
40. Not covered
44. Player's rep
46. Full court pressure
47. Capacity crowd (init.)
51. Larry Nance's alma mater (init.)
53. ___-captain
55. Dampens
58. Music disks (init.)
59. Attempt
61. Maurice Lucas' alma mater (init.)
62. A cheer
64. Go ___ guy

Solution on page 186

RETIRED UNIFORM NUMBERS

5	Dick Van Arsdale	42	Connie Hawkins
6	Walter Davis	44	Paul Westphal
33	Alvan Adams		

```
Y  H  C  H  A  M  B  E  R  S  F  O  V  J  A
M  A  N  N  I  N  G  D  S  E  I  D  A  O  V
I  W  C  F  G  Y  E  L  O  S  T  A  M  H  M
T  K  I  D  D  N  C  M  B  I  Z  V  A  N  Z
W  I  L  L  I  A  M  S  E  L  S  I  J  S  V
S  N  Y  K  W  E  S  T  R  A  I  S  E  O  A
I  S  O  E  R  I  O  M  S  S  M  L  R  N  N
B  A  L  R  A  I  N  G  E  A  M  Z  L  J  A
A  H  O  R  R  M  A  C  L  E  O  D  E  O  R
R  W  A  L  K  S  S  M  A  I  N  N  E  H  S
K  T  O  T  C  O  A  D  A  M  S  U  S  N  D
L  S  I  R  O  B  I  N  S  O  N  H  U  S  A
E  C  O  L  A  N  G  E  L  O  M  A  C  Y  L
Y  T  J  C  H  Z  V  K  P  E  R  S  O  N  E
D  W  E  S  T  P  H  A  L  L  R  T  J  B  E
```

ADAMS	JOHNSON	ROBINSON
AINGE	KERR	SILAS
BARKLEY	KIDD	SOBERS
CHAMBERS	MACLEOD	VAN ARSDALE
COLANGELO	MACY	WALK
DAVIS	MAJERLE	WEST
FITZSIMMONS	MANNING	WESTPHAL
HAWKINS	PERSON	WILLIAMS

PORTLAND TRAIL BLAZERS

The Portland basketball fans made a name for themselves. For years it was the most automatic number in the NBA: 12,666. Then it was changed to 12,888. It was more automatic than a Clyde Drexler dunk or the yearly Rose Festival. There it was again: 12,888. It was that way for every game in Portland's Memorial Coliseum from 1977–95. For 810 consecutive regular-season games— the longest streak in professional sports history—the Portland Trail Blazers filled their arena to capacity. The last time they didn't sell out a game was Apr. 5, 1977. Then in 1995–96, the Blazers moved into the new 21,300-seat, $262 million Rose Garden. The streak came to a halt, but the enthusiasm didn't wane.

The Portland crowd is fanatical, yes. But it's also had plenty to cheer about since the tail end of the 1976–77 season. That was the end of Jack Ramsay's first season as the Trail Blazers' head coach. He was hired to put life into a franchise that failed to make the playoffs or have a winning record in any of its first six seasons.

Ramsay utilized Bill Walton as the center of his offense. The big Redhead missed parts of his first two NBA seasons with injuries. But in 1976–77 he liked what Ramsay preached and rose the level of his play and the play of all the others around him. There was the enforcer, forward Maurice Lucas, and guards Lionel Hollins and Dave Twardzik. There were forwards Bob Gross and Larry Steele and a bench that knew its role.

The Blazers got off to their best start ever and were 23–12 by Jan. 1. They continued to gel, but had a five-game losing skid in February. They righted themselves and closed the season with six straight wins to finish 49–33. It was the Blazers' first appearance in the playoffs, and they made the most of it. They beat Chicago in a mini-series, 2 games to 1. Then they eliminated Midwest Division champion Denver, 4–2. The Los Angeles Lakers compiled the best regular season record and were heavy favorites over Portland in the Conference finals. But the Trail Blazers swept the Lakers, 4–0, to advance to the NBA Finals against the Philadelphia 76ers. Portland lost the first two games in Philly, but it evened the series by winning the next two in Oregon. Game 5 was set for Philadelphia where the Sixers had lost just nine times all season. Portland won behind Gross' 25 points and Walton's 24 rebounds. That gave the Blazers a 3–2 lead and sent the series back to Portland. Game 6 was tied 40–40 early in the second quarter when Portland went on a 17–2 run. Philadelphia chipped away at the Blazers' lead the rest of the way and pulled to within two points in the final seconds. The Sixers had the ball with a chance to tie, but three shots fell wide, and the entire northwest erupted as Portland won the NBA title.

The Blazers appeared ready to defend their championship in 1977–78. They were 47–10 and had their sights set on the NBA's all-time win mark when Walton was injured. Three games later, Walton's replacement, Lloyd Neal, went out with a season-ending knee injury. Portland still limped home to a league-best 58–24 record, but it was eliminated in its first round of the playoffs.

Walton missed the entire 1978–79 season with a stress fracture in his foot and signed with the San Diego Clippers when he became a free agent at the end of that season. Without Walton, the Blazers slid into the middle-of-the-pack in the standings and advanced to the second round of the playoffs only once in the next dozen years.

Rick Adelman replaced Mike Schuler as coach for the final 35 games of the 1988–89 season. The Blazers struggled to a 39–43 record that year and were swept by the Lakers in the first round of the playoffs, 3–0. But Adelman could see the makings of a good team, a very good team. The week before the college draft, the Blazers traded center Sam Bowie and their No. 1 pick in the upcoming draft for power forward Buck Williams.

The blue-collar Williams turned out to be the missing piece. With Drexler doing the scoring (23.3 points a game) and Terry Porter doing the dishing (9.1 assists a game), Williams added inside strength with Kevin Duckworth and Jerome Kersey. The Blazers compiled a record of 59–23 and advanced to the NBA Finals before losing to the Detroit Pistons, 4–1.

Portland improved to a league-best 63–19 in 1990–91, but were upset by the Lakers in the Conference finals, 4–2. The same starters stayed intact for a third straight season and compiled a 57–25 record. The Blazers advanced to the Finals again, but lost to the Chicago Bulls, 4–2.

In 1992–93, Drexler suffered a leg injury and was limited to 49 games. Kersey missed 17 games and Duckworth eight. The Blazers still were able to win 51 games, but were upset in the first round of the playoffs by the San Antonio Spurs. The Blazers' management and fans grew weary of coming up just short, so changes were in store. Slowly players were dealt, including the popular Drexler. After a 47–35 record and early elimination in the playoffs in 1994, Adelman was released and replaced with P. J. Carlesimo.

The Blazers slipped to 44 wins and were swept in the first round in 1994–95. Portland matched its 44 wins in 1995–96, but for the fourth year in a row the Blazers were eliminated in the first round of the playoffs.

The Blazers improved to 49–33 in 1996–97, but when the team failed to advance to the second round of the playoffs, Carlesimo was replaced by Mike Dunleavy. The coaching change had little impact. Portland finished with a record of 46–36 and in the playoffs—no surprise here—were beaten in the first round.

Rasheed Wallace led the Trail Blazers in blocked shots and field goal percentages in 1997–98.

INDIVIDUAL RECORDS

Career

Points: 18,040, Clyde Drexler, 1983–95

Rebounds: 5,339, Clyde Drexler, 1983–95

Assists: 5,319, Terry Porter, 1985–95

Field Goal Pct.: .550, Buck Williams, 1989–96

Free Throw Pct.: .881, Kiki Vandeweghe, 1984–89

Season

Points: 2,185, Clyde Drexler, 1987–88

Rebounds: 967, Lloyd Neal, 1972–73

Assists: 831, Terry Porter, 1987–88

Field Goal Pct.: .612, Dave Twardzik, 1976–77

Free Throw Pct.: .896, Kiki Vandeweghe, 1984–85

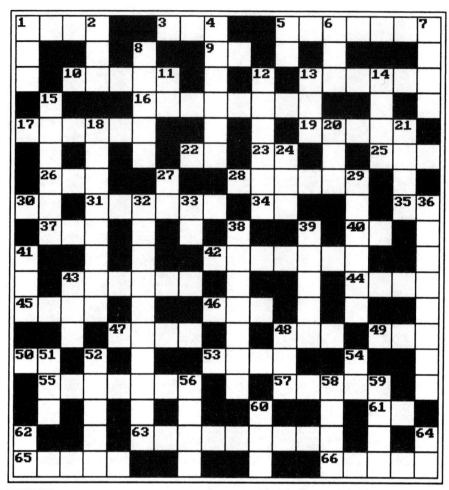

ACROSS

1. Basket
3. A team color
5. Grab a missed shot
9. Mychal Thompson's alma mater (init.)
10. Fall behind
13. Rebounds
16. Blazers' head coach
17. Leading scorer on 1st Blazers' team
19. Arm joint
22. Play-___-play announcer
23. Last column on box score (init.)
25. Tap

26. Back-up player
28. Blazers' career assists leader
30. ___ shoots, he scores!
31. Part of a sneaker
34. Column heading on roster (abbr.)
35. A cheer
37. Payment for game in Japan
40. Maurice Lucas' alma mater (init.)
42. Leading scorer on 1977–78 team
43. Blazers' pick before Jordan, and family
44. Too
45. Possible Sunday starting time

46. Point value of FT
47. Omit
48. Pass leading to a basket (abbr.)
49. End of a foot
50. Wire service (init.)
53. Blazers' 1st head coach
55. Team leader
57. Selection of college players
61. Kent Benson's alma mater (init.)
63. Starting center on '90 Finals team
65. Matches
66. Throw out of a game

DOWN

1. Smack
2. Qtr.
4. Ivy League FT bricklayer
5. Blackman's nickname
6. Crowd sound of displeasure
7. Throw a pass (slang)
8. Guard acquired in '96 trade for Robinson, Curley and 1st round pick
11. LaRue Martin's alma mater (init.)
12. NBA MVP in 1977–78
13. No game scheduled today
14. Cheer

15. Longwood College forward played 11 seasons in Portland
18. 1992–93 NBA 6th Man of the Year
20. UCLA guard Greg ___
21. Position on side of the court
24. Paid player
27. Go ___ guy
29. Hall of Fame coach was mentor of championship team
32. Blazers' single-game record holder with 20 assists, twice
33. West Coast rival (init.)
36. Foe
38. Clemon, Dave, John, Ken, Ollie or Steve
39. 1st round pick averaged 22.3 ppg in 5-year Blazers career
41. Spectator
43. Trick defense: ___-and-1
48. Stat crew compilation
51. FGM divided by FGA (abbr.)
52. Distance between players
54. Players get 6 per game (init.)
56. ___ Weatherspoon
58. Pain
59. Kept on the scoreboard
60. Ahead: on ___
62. Rod Strickland's position (init.)
64. Away

Solution on page 186

RETIRED UNIFORM NUMBERS

1	Larry Weinberg	32	Bill Walton
13	Dave Twardzik	36	Lloyd Neal
15	Larry Steele	45	Geoff Petrie
20	Maurice Lucas	77	Jack Ramsay

```
S  N  I  L  L  O  H  N  E  S  V  B  D  H  T
E  K  N  A  M  L  E  D  A  J  A  U  U  E  W
L  T  H  O  M  P  S  O  N  O  N  O  C  A  P
U  W  I  R  N  N  A  E  D  L  S  P  K  N  O
Y  A  S  M  A  R  A  R  E  G  O  A  W  S  R
C  L  S  B  O  L  E  A  R  B  N  X  O  C  T
S  T  A  B  G  R  V  K  S  B  L  S  R  H  E
L  O  A  R  R  Y  I  L  O  A  Z  O  T  U  R
U  N  O  E  N  Z  U  W  N  G  R  N  H  L  I
C  S  D  G  D  C  I  T  S  T  E  E  L  E  L
S  I  T  R  A  E  K  L  O  N  L  E  N  R  L
R  O  A  S  Y  E  L  D  U  D  X  T  I  L  O
N  W  G  B  R  Y  D  S  M  Y  E  S  R  E  K
T  P  S  M  A  I  L  L  I  W  R  S  O  R  E
R  E  I  R  T  E  P  M  I  S  D  L  B  A  C
```

ADELMAN	HOLLINS	RIDER
ANDERSON	KERSEY	SCHULER
BOWIE	LUCAS	STEELE
DREXLER	NEAL	THOMPSON
DUCKWORTH	PAXSON	TODD
DUDLEY	PETRIE	TWARDZIK
DUNLEAVY	PORTER	WALTON
GROSS	RAMSAY	WILLIAMS

SACRAMENTO KINGS

No one has taken the words of Horace Greeley more literally than the Sacramento Kings. It was in a New York Tribune editorial that Greeley offered the advice, "Go west, young man!" The Kings' franchise began in Rochester, N.Y., moved to Cincinnati, Ohio, in 1957, Kansas City, Mo., in 1972 and Sacramento, Calif., in 1985. Can Honolulu and Tokyo be far away?

The Rochester Royals began play in the NBA in 1948–49 after competing in the National Basketball League for three years. They were an immediate success, compiling the best record at 45–15. But they were eliminated in the playoffs in the Division finals. The following season they tied for the most wins, but were upset in the opening round of the playoffs.

Finally, in 1950–51 the Royals got post-season play figured out and won the title. They finished in second place in the Western Division under Coach Les Harrison, but breezed through the first two rounds of the playoffs. In the championship series they beat their intra-state rival New York Knickerbockers in seven games. Arnold Risen, Robert Davies and Bob Wanzer were the key players during that era.

The Royals remained competitive until they moved to Cincinnati prior to the 1957–58 season. By then Wanzer had taken over the coaching duties and was relying on all-stars Jack Twyman and Maurice Stokes. That would be Stokes' final season. He was paralyzed from posttraumatic encephalopathy suffered from hitting his head on the floor during a game. The Royals found Stokes hard to replace. They slipped to 19 wins in back-to-back seasons and didn't fully recover until 1960–61 when they obtained local college all-American Oscar Robertson. In his rookie season, the "Big O" nearly averaged a triple double: 30.5 points, 10.1 rebounds and 9.7 assists per game.

In 10 years in Cincinnati, Robertson averaged nearly 30 points a game. He was named to the all-star team 10 times and was named the league's MVP in 1963–64. That was the year the Royals peaked at 55–25, yet still couldn't get past the dominant Boston Celtics.

Robertson's supporting cast began to deteriorate and the team began a long, steady decline. Former Celtics great Bob Cousy was named the head coach in 1969–70 and sparked the team briefly, but as the Royals' slide continued, interest in Cincinnati diminished. It was at the end of the 1969–70 season that the Royals made a pair of significant transactions. First, they traded Robertson to the Milwaukee Bucks for Flynn Robinson and Charlie Paulk. Then they used their second-round pick in the college draft to select a "tiny" guard from Texas–El Paso, Nate Archibald.

In the summer of 1972, the Royals moved to Kansas City–Omaha and became known as the Kings. They played part of their home schedule at the Municipal Auditorium in Kansas City, and part at the Omaha Civic Auditorium 190 miles away.

It was that first season in K.C.–Omaha that Archibald caught the national spotlight. He had been impressive in his rookie season of 1970–71, scoring 16 points a game. The entire league perked up when he scored 28 points per contest in Year Two. But his third season remains one for the records books. He led the NBA in scoring with 34.0 points a game and also led the league in assists with 11.4 per game. That's a feat that no other player, before or after, has been able to accomplish.

Cousy was replaced during the 1973–74 season by Phil Johnson. The fiery new coach put life into the Kings and in 1974–75 they went 44–38 and qualified for the playoffs for the first time in eight seasons. For his efforts, Johnson received a league-leading 34 technical fouls and NBA Coach of the Year honors.

In the summer of 1975, the club changed its name to just "Kansas City Kings," even though it still continued to play a handful of games each season in Omaha. Johnson's voracity quickly wore off and he was replaced in 1978. Cotton Fitzsimmons guided the Kings to a 48–34 mark in 1978–79, and he also won the NBA Coach of the Year award. In 1980–81, the Kings finished 40–42 and advanced to the Conference finals before losing to the Houston Rockets, 4 games to 2.

That's the last time the Kings won a playoff series. They've made the playoffs only three times in 17 years since then, and their appearance in 1996 was the first in 10 years.

The Kings moved from Kansas City to Sacramento in the summer of 1985. Even though the fans have witnessed just three home playoff game (all losses), every seat to nearly every home game has been filled. The Kings were in the playoffs in their first year at Sacramento after a 37–45 record, but then went nine straight years without getting into post-season play. The Kings went through six coaches before settling on Garry St. Jean. They improved their record in each his first four seasons, but when the team began the 1996–97 season 28–39, he was replaced by Eddie Jordan.

Under Jordan, the Kings wound up 27–55 in 1997–98, despite the continued efforts on the court of Mitch Richmond, Corliss Williamson and Billy Owens.

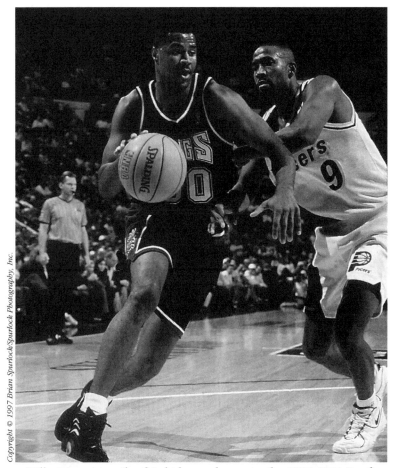

Billy Owens was the third player chosen in the 1991 NBA Draft.

INDIVIDUAL RECORDS

Career

      Points: 22,009, Oscar Robertson, 1960–70

      Rebounds: 9,353, Sam Lacey, 1970–82

      Assists: 7,731, Oscar Robertson, 1960–70

      Field Goal Pct.: .604, Steve Johnson, 1981–84

      Free Throw Pct.: .862, Spud Webb, 1991–95

Season

      Points: 2,719, Nate Archibald, 1972–73

      Rebounds: 1,668, Jerry Lucas, 1965–66

      Assists: 910, Nate Archibald, 1972–73

      Field Goal Pct.: .624, Steve Johnson, 1982–83

      Free Throw Pct.: .934, Spud Webb, 1994–95

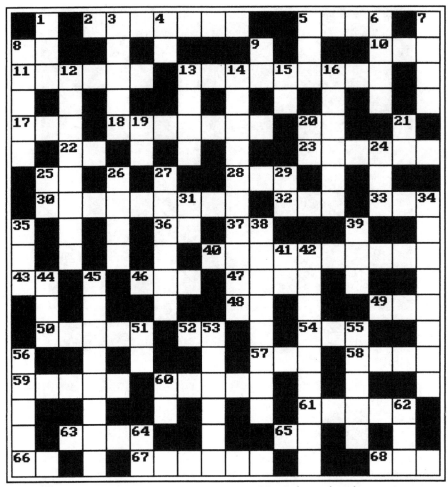

ACROSS

2. Kings' head coach and Michael
5. Fills a sneaker
8. Throw away a pass (abbr.)
10. Take away a pass (abr.)
11. Duke guard injured in auto accident
13. Original home of Kings' franchise
17. Alex Hannum's alma mater (init.)
18. 1st round pick in '90 from LaSalle played 7 years in Sacramento
20. Play-___-play announcer
22. Column heading on roster (abbr.)
23. Adrian, Derek, Don, Kenny, LaBradford and Michael
28. Treatment for sprained ankle
30. The Big O
32. Fastbreak
33. Qtr.
36. Extra period (abbr.)
37. Ray Ragelis' alma mater (init.)
40. Kings' previous home
43. ___ vs. Them
46. Basket cord
47. Arena section
48. Royals still in Cincy: What ___?

49. Capacity crowd (init.)
50. Narrow roadway between buildings
52. Before Gee, Daniel or Mahon
54. Smack
57. Baseball stat (init.)
58. Grab
59. Signal end of periods
60. Ricochet
61. Stadium
63. Metal rim
65. Rodney McCray's alma mater (init.)
66. Logo registration (abbr.)
67. Rebounds
68. Month for training camp (abbr.)

DOWN

1. 6th man salute: Thank ___, fans!
3. Forward acquired in '96 trade with Gamble for Williams and Corbin
4. ___ or die
5. 1-pointers
6. Grow weary
7. Make a defensive stand
8. Set Kings' record with 18 assists in '86 game
9. 1st word of the national anthem
12. Member of 1988 and '96 U.S. Olympic teams
13. Hoops
14. Franchise's home, 1957–72
15. Former

16. No. 2 on franchise's career scoring list with 15,840 points from 1955–66
19. Roster spot for hurt players (init.)
20. Rejection (init.)
21. Otis Birdsong's alma mater (init.)
24. Tip
25. Publicity (init.)
26. Spud
27. Had 38 rebounds in '56 game
29. Where severely injured players are sent (init.)
31. Take away the ball (abbr.)
34. Dir. of Player Personnel was twice the team's interim head coach
35. Jerry Lucas' alma mater (init.)
38. Jerseys and shorts
39. FGM divided by FGA (abbr.)
41. Football receiver (pos.)
42. Led league in scoring and assists in same season
44. Whirlpool
45. A division
51. Column heading on roster (abbr.)
53. Player's tenure
55. Mahmoud Abdul-Rauf's uniform number
56. Attempt to score
60. ___-captain
62. 3-pt. line
64. Column heading on standings (init.)

Solution on page 187

RETIRED UNIFORM NUMBERS

1	Nate Archibald	14	Oscar Robertson
6	Sixth Man (fan)	27	Jack Twyman
11	Bob Davies	44	Sam Lacey
12	Maurice Stokes		

```
G  E  I  B  T  M  O  D  N  O  M  H  C  I  R
V  L  L  E  S  S  U  R  O  M  B  B  I  R  W
C  A  S  N  O  M  M  I  S  S  N  E  W  O  Y
E  B  N  A  S  E  A  O  E  N  A  E  J  T  S
L  N  A  M  D  E  W  R  T  W  E  M  T  H  A
A  T  I  Y  Y  G  O  H  E  N  A  D  R  O  J
D  I  A  W  K  R  E  B  T  D  V  E  U  R  E
S  S  I  T  O  U  B  Y  E  L  R  U  H  N  C
I  S  N  A  S  S  O  M  D  A  A  B  V  O  I
T  A  O  Y  E  C  A  L  E  B  S  I  A  S  N
M  C  S  E  K  O  T  S  N  I  E  Z  I  I  Y
M  U  N  E  H  E  P  R  O  H  T  I  T  R  L
T  L  H  W  I  Y  S  U  O  C  S  A  E  R  O
S  N  O  S  T  R  E  B  O  R  H  S  W  A  P
B  L  J  C  E  S  E  I  V  A  D  N  H  H  J
```

ARCHIBALD	LACEY	ST. JEAN
COUSY	LUCAS	STOKES
DAVIES	OWENS	THEUS
EMBRY	POLYNICE	THORPE
HARRISON	RICHMOND	TISDALE
HURLEY	ROBERTSON	TWYMAN
JOHNSON	RUSSELL	WEBB
JORDAN	SIMMONS	WEDMAN

SAN ANTONIO SPURS

The Iceman and The Admiral. George Gervin and David Robinson. The glorious, gold-plated bookends to the Spurs' NBA history.

When the Spurs gained entry into the NBA in the summer of 1976, it was Gervin who gave them immediate respectability. Coming from the American Basketball Association, the Spurs and Gervin erased all doubts about the level of competition in the red, white and blue basketball league. They went 44–38 in their first season in the senior circuit, then won their division in five of the next six seasons. Gervin, meanwhile, led the NBA in scoring four times in his first six years in the league.

On the other end of the spectrum, Robinson has established himself as one of the great players in the game today. An eight-time all-star and a member of three Olympic teams, the Naval Ensign has led the Spurs to four Midwest Division titles and three runners-up.

But in between Gervin and Robinson, there was little to cheer about.

Despite those division titles, the Spurs never have made it to the NBA Finals. In 1983–84 they began a slide which lasted for six years. It reached its low point in 1988–89 when the Spurs went 21–61 under first-year coach Larry Brown. But despite the dismal finish, optimism ran rampant throughout the organization. It was two years earlier that San Antonio had used a Red Chameleon good luck charm to draw the No. 1 spot in the draft lottery. That pick turned out to be Robinson. The only problem was that he was required to fulfill a two-year Navy obligation before he could begin his pro basketball career.

Robinson signed a contract and went on active duty at Kings Point, Ga. There was concern about what a two-year layoff from competitive hoops would do, but those concerns were quickly erased at the start of the 1989–90 season. Robinson wasn't the only new face at training camp that year. The Spurs went through a complete make-over, adding Terry Cummings from Milwaukee, Maurice Cheeks, Christian Welp and David Wingate from Philadelphia, and signing free agents Caldwell Jones and Zarko Paspalj. In addition, Sean Elliott, an all-American at Arizona, was selected in the first round of the 1989 college draft.

San Antonio lost two of its first three games, but then began winning on a regular basis. The Spurs were 19–7 by New Year's Day and 32–14 at the all-star break. They won their final seven games to go 56–26, a 35-win improvement over the previous season, the highest increase of victories from one season to the next of any NBA team in history. Robinson was the consensus

Rookie of the Year, averaging 24.3 points, 12.0 rebounds and 3.89 blocked shots a game. Yet, the Spurs were beaten in the second round of the playoffs by the Portland Trail Blazers, 4 games to 3.

In 1990–91, the Spurs won the Midwest Division again, going 55–27, but they lost to the Golden State Warriors in the first round of the playoffs. In 1991–92, Brown was replaced unexpectedly 38 games into the season. Long-time General Manager Bob Bass took over as an interim coach for the fourth time in his career and guided the club to a 47–35 record. The Spurs again failed to advance in the playoffs, losing in three straight games to the Phoenix Suns.

In the summer of 1992, the Spurs hired Jerry Tarkanian, the embittered UNLV coach who had ongoing battles with the NCAA and his school administration. A lack of experience in the professional game was too much to overcome and he was replaced a month into the season. Former Spur John Lucas was named the head coach and provided new enthusiasm and confidence to the Spurs. They wound up 49–33 (after a 9–11 start), beat Portland in the first round of the playoffs and lost to Phoenix in Round Two.

In 1993–94 the Spurs moved into the new Alamodome with the set-up for basketball seating 20,500. They had played in the HemisFair Arena (16,057 capacity) which was known for having its roof raised to install additional seats in the upper deck.

The Spurs were 55–27 in 1993–94, but when they were eliminated in the first round of the playoffs, Lucas was replaced by Bob Hill. Hill led the Spurs to two straight division titles, but still no Finals berths. After the team started 3–15 in 1996–97 (with Robinson injured), he was replaced by Gregg Popovich. Robinson's injury was a blessing in disguise. It allowed the Spurs to gain the No. 1 pick in the 1997 draft. They used it to select Wake Forest's Tim Duncan, who wound up the NBA Rookie of the Year. Behind the duo of Robinson (21.6 ppg) and Duncan (21.1 ppg), the Spurs finished 56–26. They were eliminated in the second round of the playoffs.

The franchise had its beginning as the Dallas Chaparrals in the American Basketball Association in 1967–68. They finished 46–32 that first season. In 1970–71 the name was changed to the "Texas Chaparrals," as they split their home schedule to include games in Dallas, Ft. Worth and Lubbock. That experiment didn't work and they went back to being the Dallas Chaparrals in 1971–72.

After dropping to 28–56 in 1972–73, the franchise was sold and moved to San Antonio. The nickname was changed to "Spurs." The change of scenery helped. The Spurs improved to 45–39 in 1973–74 and 51–33 in 1974–75. In the final year of operations in the ABA, the Spurs were 50–34 and finished in third place. It was in the summer of 1976 that the Spurs joined three other ABA teams in going to the NBA.

David Robinson was the NBA's Most Valuable Player in 1995.

INDIVIDUAL RECORDS
Career
> Points: 19,383, George Gervin, 1976–85
>
> Rebounds: 7,389, David Robinson, 1989–98
>
> Assists: 3,865, Johnny Moore, 1980–88, 1989–90
>
> Field Goal Pct.: .620, Artis Gilmore, 1982–87
>
> Free Throw Pct.: .861, Johnny Dawkins, 1986–89

Season
> Points: 2,585, George Gervin, 1983–84
>
> Rebounds: 1,367, Dennis Rodman, 1993–94
>
> Assists: 816, Johnny Moore, 1984–85
>
> Field Goal Pct.: .632, Steve Johnson, 1985–86
>
> Free Throw Pct.: .896, Johnny Dawkins, 1987–88

ACROSS

1. Official's hand gesture
4. N.C. St. guard has collection of more than 300 movies
9. A cheer
10. Edge
11. The lane
13. 4-time interim head coach for the Spurs
16. Get beaten
19. Pain
20. Virginia guard averaged in double-digits in 1985–86
23. Swat
24. The Admiral
25. Column heading on stat sheet (init.)
27. ___ and in
29. Wager on a game
30. Excitement
33. Texas guard missed quadruple double by just 1 steal in '85 game
34. Column heading on roster (abbr.)
35. ___-announcer (init.)
36. Arena signs
37. He ___ Game
38. All-star forward has more than 100 fish, 6 snakes and 2 lizards
40. Uniform number of John Paxson

42. Basket
44. Before Kenzie or Namara
47. Computation for stat crew
48. Column heading on roster (abbr.)
49. Fruit drink
53. John Shumate's university (init.)
54. Jacksonville southpaw had 700 BS in 5 years
55. Aide
58. Willie Anderson's alma mater (init.)
59. ___ and out
60. Extra period (abbr.)
61. Spurs' division
63. Carom at own basket (init.)
64. Rejection (init.)
65. Regulations
67. Cadillac
68. Ref's relative

DOWN

1. NBC game day
2. Open area
3. Ahead
4. 1997–98 NBA Rookie of the Year
5. West Coast rival (init.)
6. Former
7. NBA steals leader in 1985–86 and 1986–87
8. 2-pointers (init.)
12. ___-___ record (init.)
14. Back-up player

15. Spurs' career scoring leader
17. Off the court (init.)
18. 3.4 apg, .564 or 5 PF
20. Sass
21. William Bedford's alma mater (init.)
22. Spurs' head coach
26. Attempt to score
28. Ken, Larry or Robert
29. Defeat
31. Team symbol
32. Jason Kidd's alma mater (abbr.)
35. Has 2 horses, named Pepsi and Magic, and 3 championship rings
39. Ahead: ___ top
41. Sean Elliott's alma mater (init.)
43. Spurs' TV announcer
44. Coach
45. Arena music maker
46. Texas rival
50. Set Spurs record with 1,367 rebounds in 1993–94
51. Basketball players (slang)
52. Come out ahead
56. Rest on the bench
57. Championship
58. Christian Welp's alma mater (init.)
62. Do or ___
63. Steve Johnson's alma mater (init.)
64. Play-___-play announcer
66. Wire service

Solution on page 187

RETIRED UNIFORM NUMBERS

13	James Silas
44	George Gervin

```
S  T  T  I  D  E  L  N  E  G  R  O  D  R  J
O  A  E  N  O  O  B  N  O  S  N  I  B  O  R
J  A  C  D  I  N  S  K  K  J  O  M  H  H  N
O  O  I  U  J  O  O  E  C  N  O  N  I  A  M
B  U  T  L  L  S  N  N  E  E  S  L  T  L  O
A  R  T  N  A  D  O  S  E  O  B  E  E  R  R
W  A  O  L  S  I  S  S  N  K  R  L  Z  O  E
K  S  I  W  V  E  R  N  O  T  H  O  A  Y  D
I  S  L  R  N  T  E  M  I  I  C  I  L  S  R
N  K  L  O  I  R  D  M  L  S  I  B  T  N  O
S  G  E  R  V  I  N  L  S  O  V  R  A  I  D
E  R  O  O  M  C  A  A  R  B  O  E  B  K  M
S  Z  V  O  B  K  B  R  E  R  P  N  B  W  A
N  A  C  N  U  D  G  I  L  M  O  R  E  A  N
N  T  T  B  I  E  U  D  R  E  P  A  E  D  O
```

ALBECK	DUNCAN	MOE
ANDERSON	ELLIOTT	MOORE
BASS	GERVIN	NATER
BOONE	GILMORE	PERDUE
BROWN	HILL	POPOVICH
DAWKINS	JOHNSON	ROBINSON
DEL NEGRO	KENON	RODMAN
DIETRICK	LUCAS	SILAS

SEATTLE SUPERSONICS

The city of Seattle was awarded an NBA franchise on Dec. 20, 1966. Sam Schulman headed the first ownership group. The first general manager was Don Richman and the first coach was Al Bianchi. The first player chosen in the expansion draft of NBA players was Tom Meschery from the San Francisco Warriors. The first player selected in the 1967 college draft was forward Al Tucker of Oklahoma Baptist.

The SuperSonics played their first game on Oct. 13, 1967, at San Francisco and the SuperSonics lost, 144–116. Seattle's first win was Oct. 21 at San Diego over the Rockets, 117–100, in overtime.

Bianchi coached the Sonics for two seasons. Lenny Wilkens became a player/coach in 1969–70 and served in that capacity until he was traded (as a player) to Cleveland in the summer of 1972. Tom Nissalke took over, but was replaced with 22 games remaining in his first season by Bucky Buckwalter. Bill Russell was named coach (and general manager) in 1973–74. He was replaced by Bob Hopkins prior to the 1977–78 season. The Sonics were just 5–17 under Hopkins when Wilkens was re-hired (this time just as a coach) in 1977–78. Wilkens left following the 1984–85 season and Bernie Bickerstaff got the call. He lasted five seasons and was replaced by K. C. Jones prior to the 1990–91 campaign. Jones was replaced after a year and a half by Bob Kloppenburg (four games) and then George Karl, who was there until the summer of 1998. He was replaced by Paul Westphal.

The Sonics were in their eighth season before they qualified for the playoffs. Since then, they've made the playoffs 19 times in 24 years.

Seattle won the Pacific Division in 1978–79 with a 52–30 mark. Then they went 56–26 in 1979–80. In 1993–94 the Sonics won the Division with a league-best 63–19 mark. They followed that with 57 wins in 1994–95 and three more Division titles: 1995–96 (64–18), 1996–97 (57–25) and 1997–98 (61–21, tied for first).

The Sonics advanced to the NBA Finals in 1977–78 despite their third-place finish in the Pacific Division. They started the season 5–17 under Hopkins, but then Wilkens was brought in. He guided Seattle to a 42–18 mark the rest of the way. They beat the Los Angeles Lakers in the first round of the playoffs, 2 games to 1, then got by the Portland Trail Blazers, 4–2. In the Western Conference finals, they eliminated the Denver Nuggets, 4–2. The Sonics faced the Washington Bullets in the Finals. Seattle took a 3–2 lead in the series. Game 6 was in Washington and the Bullets won, 117–82. The series returned to the

Seattle Center Coliseum for Game 7 where the Sonics had won 22 straight games. The Bullets built an eight-point halftime lead and extended that to 13 after three quarters. The Sonics waged a comeback attempt in the fourth period, but fell short, losing, 105–99.

The following season, the Sonics returned to the Finals and again faced the Bullets. Washington won the opening game, but then the Sonics reeled off four straight wins (two of them on the Bullets' home floor) to win their only NBA title. Gus Williams led the team in scoring in each contest (he averaged 28.6 points a game in the series), but Dennis Johnson, who starred at both ends of the court, was named the series MVP.

The Sonics got back to the NBA Finals in 1995–96, but lost to the Chicago Bulls, 4 games to 2.

Seattle long will be remembered as being involved in one of the most controversial signings in league history. On Dec. 30, 1970, Schulman defied the NBA's four-year collegiate eligibility rule and signed Spencer Haywood to a contract. At the time, there was no "hardship" rule or waiving of college eligibility to play in the NBA. The American Basketball Association allowed undergraduates to sign, and Haywood left the University of Detroit after his sophomore season to sign with Denver in the ABA. After a season there, Haywood wanted to play in the NBA. The courts finally OK'd the Sonics' offer and said the NBA had to let players enter the draft if they desired, even if they hadn't completed four years in college.

And some of the wackiest stories in the Sonics' history involve the Seattle Center Coliseum. It was built at a cost of $4.5 million to house Washington's "World of Tomorrow" exhibit for the 1962 World's Fair. In 1972, Haywood almost saw his career end when he slipped on a wet floor, caused by the leaky roof, and injured a knee ligament. In 1986, after more than $2 million was spent to refurbish the building, the NBA's first "Postponed due to rain" game was played. A game was delayed to make repairs to the leaky roof and was completed the following day. But the best story about the Coliseum occurred during the 1970s. The ceiling rises from 14 feet on the outside to 80 feet in the middle. The slope of the ceiling inspired a Nordic ski jumping competition. Enthusiasts hauled in snow from outlying areas, built a ramp jump and managed to survive the competition with no major mishaps. The Coliseum underwent a major facelift to the tune of $119 million during 1994–95. (The Sonics played the entire season in Tacoma.) When it re-opened for the 1995–96 season, it was dubbed the Key Arena and has a capacity of 17,100 for basketball.

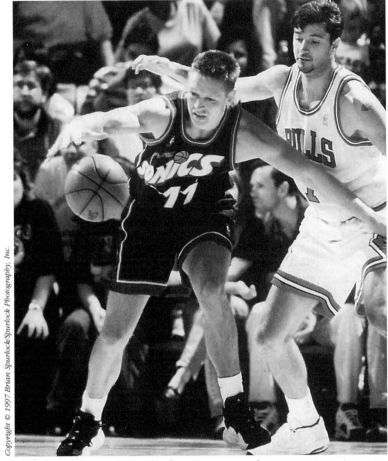

Copyright © 1997 Brian Spurlock/Spurlock Photography, Inc.

Detlef Schrempf was the first European player to appear in an NBA All-Star Game.

INDIVIDUAL RECORDS

Career

Points: 14,018, Fred Brown, 1971–84

Rebounds: 7,729, Jack Sikma, 1977–86

Assists: 4,893, Nate McMillan, 1986–98

Field Goal Pct.: .584, James Donaldson, 1980–83

Free Throw Pct.: .906, Ricky Pierce, 1990–94

Season

Points: 2,253, Dale Ellis, 1988–89

Rebounds: 1,038, Jack Sikma, 1981–82

Assists: 766, Lenny Wilkens, 1971–72

Field Goal Pct.: .609, James Donaldson, 1981–82

Free Throw Pct.: .925, Ricky Pierce, 1990–91

ACROSS

1. 1-shot foul
5. Athletic supporter
8. Front office head (init.)
9. Tip
12. Sass
14. Carom at own basket (init.)
15. Rebounds
16. X
19. Promissory note (init.)
20. ___ and out
21. 1st underclassman to play in NBA
24. Talk with the ref
26. Come out ahead
28. Column heading on standings (init.)
29. Kendall Gill's alma mater (init.)
30. Newspaper head (abbr.)
32. Alton Lister's college state (abbr.)
35. Squad
37. Mourning's nickname
38. USC guard led Sonics in scoring 5 seasons
40. Tim McCormick's alma mater (init.)
42. Last column on box score (init.)
43. TV talk: ___, Mom!
44. Dale Ellis' alma mater (init.)
45. Sonics' head coach, 1992–98

46. Walk with a sore leg

48. Knot

49. Guard acquired from Bucks for Dale Ellis in '91 trade

51. All right

53. Arm joint

56. Colorado St. forward was an all-star and team scoring leader in 1969–70

57. 1995–96 NBA Defensive Player of the Year

60. Players who begin the game

62. Sonics' career rebounding leader

65. Column heading on roster (abbr.)

66. ___ or die

67. Full court pressure

69. ___ shoots, he scores!

70. Sprain, twist or spasm

71. Usual college class of draftees

DOWN

1. Logo registration

2. Grabbing

3. ___-captain

4. Are ahead

5. Avery, Clemon, Dennis, Eddie, Ervin, John, Steve or Vinnie

6. Recorded 2 20–20 games in '90

7. ___ and in

9. Throw the ball away (abbr.)

10. Stadium

11. Spectator

13. 1-on-1

15. Downtown Freddie

17. Basketball's minor league (init.)

18. West Coast rival (init.)

21. Became Abdul-Rahman

22. Marv Albert's call

23. Dave Corzine's alma mater (init.)

25. The Human Eraser

27. Basket cord

31. Discourage

33. Dunk

34. Slick

36. Wire service

38. Head coach of 1979 championship team

39. Greg Graham's alma mater (init.)

41. Type of x ray (init.)

45. All-star forward traded for Vin Baker

47. Paid player

49. Quarters

50. Set Sonics record with 2,253 points in 1988–89

52. Take the ball away (abbr.)

54. Time out drink

55. Spins

58. Column heading on roster (abbr.)

59. Tommy Kron's alma mater (init.)

61. Tap

63. Treatment for sprained ankle

64. Possible long distance shoot-out sponsor

65. Norton Barnhill's alma mater (init.)

67. Publicity (init.)

68. Former

Solution on page 188

RETIRED UNIFORM NUMBERS

19	Lenny Wilkens
32	Fred Brown
43	Jack Sikma

```
S  K  L  N  E  M  P  H  J  N  R  P  K  P  P
B  R  R  A  O  N  I  E  I  U  O  K  M  I  R
I  F  E  A  M  S  O  L  G  S  L  T  E  U  S
C  R  P  B  H  K  N  T  R  A  K  R  Y  I  H
S  I  E  M  M  E  I  H  L  B  C  E  K  A  S
D  N  S  C  E  A  L  S  O  E  E  M  W  I  P
M  O  E  S  L  R  H  E  M  J  H  K  L  D  A
W  E  N  K  L  L  H  C  I  I  I  S  E  E  I
H  I  S  A  L  A  M  C  Z  N  R  L  D  M  L
E  T  L  C  L  I  H  N  S  U  A  O  R  Z  P
L  S  Y  L  L  D  W  P  S  S  O  D  G  A  R
T  H  E  L  I  O  S  S  T  W  I  R  C  E  K
O  A  A  N  R  A  E  O  Y  S  U  L  K  M  C
N  N  T  B  O  L  M  A  N  L  E  A  L  L  T
R  U  S  N  L  J  H  S  E  H  B  W  M  E  W
```

BAKER	JOHNSON	RULE
BROWN	JONES	RUSSELL
CAGE	KARL	SCHREMPF
CHAMBERS	KEMP	SHELTON
DONALDSON	MCDANIEL	SIKMA
ELLIS	MCMILLAN	WESTPHAL
HAWKINS	PAYTON	WILKENS
HAYWOOD	PIERCE	WILLIAMS

TORONTO RAPTORS

The city of Toronto has a storied history in the National Basketball Association. It had one of the original teams in the NBA in 1946—the Toronto Huskies. It was involved in what today is recognized as the first game in league history (against the New York Knicks). The Huskies wound up with a 22–38 record. The team folded after a year. The Buffalo Braves then played 16 regular season games in Toronto from 1971–75.

It was Apr. 23, 1993, when the NBA announced it had received a formal application for expansion from Professional Basketball Franchise (Canada), Inc. (PBF), comprised of John I. Bitove, Allan Slaight, Borden Osmak, Phil Granovsky and former Ontario Premier, David Peterson, to get professional basketball back to Toronto.

Three months later, members of the NBA's expansion committee visited Toronto to meet with representatives of PBF. Two months after that, the committee announced its recommendation that PBF be awarded an expansion franchise for the 1995–96 season to become the 28th team in the NBA and the first expansion franchise outside of the U.S. It became official Nov. 4, 1993, when the NBA Board of Governors approved. The price tag was $125 million.

PBF embarked on finding the appropriate team nickname. A series of media contests netted more than 2,000 possible names. The top 10 list was dominated by animals: Beavers, Bobcats, Dragons, Grizzlies, Hogs, Raptors, Scorpions, T-Rex, Tarantulas and Terriers. On May 15, 1994, "Raptors" was chosen, along with the team colors: Raptor Red, Purple, Black and Naismith Silver. (Canadian-born Dr. James Naismith, the original Dr. J, invented the game of basketball in Massachusetts in 1891.) The snazzy logo and uniforms, complete with a dinosaur's footprint, soon put the Raptors among the top 10 teams in the league for merchandise sales—before they had ever played a game.

With those formalities completed, the Raptors set out to build a team. Isiah Thomas was named Vice President, Basketball Operations, and Brendan Malone was named the first head coach. A short time later, John Shumate, Darrell Walker and Bob Zuffelato were named assistant coaches.

On June 24, 1995, the Raptors participated in the expansion draft. They chose 14 NBA veterans: B. J. Armstrong, Tony Massenburg, Andres Guibert, Keith Jennings, Dontonio Wingfield, Doug Smith, Jerome Kersey, Zan Tabak, Willie Anderson, Ed Pinckney, Acie Earl, B. J. Tyler, John Salley and Oliver Miller.

A week later, Toronto used the seventh overall pick in the NBA's college draft to get 5-foot-10 guard Damon Stoudamire of Arizona. Jimmy King of Michigan was chosen in the second round.

Before the season began, the Raptors traded Armstrong to the Golden State Warriors for Carlos Rogers, Victor Alexander and three draft picks. In addition, veteran guard Alvin Robertson and forward Tracy Murray were signed as free agents.

The Raptors opened their inaugural season Nov. 3, 1995, at home against the New Jersey Nets. Playing in front of a SkyDome crowd of 33,306, the Raptors' starting line-up included Rogers, Pinckney, Tabak, Stoudamire and Robertson. It was Robertson who scored the club's first basket, a three-pointer 18 seconds into the game. Toronto led most of the way in winning, 94–79, to become the first expansion team to win its debut since the 1980 Dallas Mavericks.

But the opening night euphoria turned to stark reality when the Raptors lost their next seven games. Then they won three straight contests (including a 102–97 win over eventual NBA finalist Seattle). The Raptors were 8–20 by Christmas and 14–34 on Valentine's Day. They finished 21–61, six wins better than the other new expansion team, Vancouver, and three wins better than long-time NBA team, Philadelphia.

Stoudamire was an instant success. His quickness broke down defenses on fast breaks, as well as in the half-court. He wound up averaging 19.0 points and 9.3 assists per game. He had 133 three-pointers and logged more than 40 minutes a night. He was named the NBA's Rookie of the Year.

It was Stoudamire's minutes, though, that ultimately led to the departure of Malone. Thomas felt that Stoudamire was playing way too many minutes, even for an eager rookie. When Malone didn't agree, he was replaced. Walker was named the new head coach for the 1996–97 season. The Raptors snared the No. 2 overall pick in the 1996 college draft and tabbed 6-foot-11 Marcus Camby from Massachusetts.

Stoudamire again showed flashes of brilliance (20.2 points and 8.8 assists per game), but ironically, he again averaged more than 40 minutes a night. He received help from Walt Williams (16.4 ppg), Camby (14.8 ppg, 130 blocked shots), and Doug Christie (14.5 ppg). The Raptors won their final two games to finish 30–52, better than seven other teams.

High expectations soon turned sour. The Raptors selected unproved high schooler Tracy McGrady with their first round draft pick. Bickering between the Raptors and cross-town Toronto Maple Leafs of the National Hockey League over a new arena reached a feverish pitch. Then a public battle over ownership of the Raptors spilled into the media. In the end, Thomas departed.

The off-the-court problems found their way onto the court. Walker was replaced on the sidelines by Butch Carter. It all added up to a less than expected season. The Raptors used 24 different players and finished the 1997–98 season 16–66. Stoudamire, the future of the franchise, was dealt to Portland at mid-season. The lone bright spot was Camby leading the league in blocked shots with 3.65 per game.

The Raptors used their first-round pick in the 1998 college draft to select North Carolina's Antawn Jamison. But they traded him to Golden State moments later in exchange for the draft rights to North Carolina's Vince Carter and an undisclosed sum of cash.

Doug Christie is the Raptors' career steals leader.

INDIVIDUAL RECORDS

Career

Points: 3,917, Damon Stoudamire, 1995–98

Rebounds: 956, Doug Christie, 1996–98

Assists: 1,761, Damon Stoudamire, 1995–98

Field Goal Pct.: .508, Zan Tabak, 1995–98

Free Throw Pct.: .856, Willie Anderson, 1995–96

Season

Points: 1,634, Damon Stoudamire, 1996–97

Rebounds: 680, Popeye Jones, 1996–97

Assists: 709, Damon Stoudamire, 1996–97

Field Goal Pct.: .543, Zan Tabak, 1995–96

Free Throw Pct.: .844, Damon Stoudamire, 1997–98

ACROSS

5. 2-pointers (init.)
8. Part of a ticket
11. Raptors' 1st GM
13. Croatian center
15. Xs and ___
16. Back muscle (abbr.)
18. ___ shoots, he scores!
19. High school draftee
22. Swap
23. Jerry Sloan's alma mater (init.)
24. Carom at own basket (init.)
25. Raptors' head coach
28. Coach: Do it or ___!

29. Maryland forward known as The Wizard
30. Rookie to coach: Yes, ___!
32. Defeat
33. On the back of a uniform (abbr.)
35. Painted stripe
36. Column heading on roster (abbr.)
37. Roster spot for hurt players (init.)
40. Grow weary
42. In and ___
43. UCLA forward led team in 3-pointers in 1995–96, and family
46. Smack

47. Rest on the bench
48. Possible college class of early-entry candidate (abbr.)
49. Make a mistake (abbr.)
50. Up and ___
51. Play me or trade ___!
52. Clifford Rozier's alma mater (init.)
54. Edge out: win by a ___
56. Groups of fans
57. ___-captain
58. Basket cord
60. Tip
61. Doug Christie's alma mater (init.)
62. Off-road truck (init.)
65. Guard
66. Watches the next opponent
67. Herb Williams' alma mater (init.)

DOWN

1. Benoit Benjamin's alma mater (init.)
2. 1995–96 NBA Rookie of the Year
3. Personal, technical or flagrant
4. Raptors' head coach, 1996–98
6. Men's only party
7. Stomach muscle (abbr.)
9. Deadlock
10. Rebound
12. Texas rival (init.)
14. Guard selected from San Antonio in expansion draft
17. Logo registration (abbr.)
18. Type of shot
20. Led Raptors with 1,287 points in 1997–98
21. Played in '93 World University Games, 10th of 12 children in his family
23. Damon Stoudamire's alma mater (init.)
25. NBA leader in blocked shots in 1997–98
26. Kept on the scoreboard
27. Raptors' career rebounding leader, and family
31. Titleist
34. Toronto's province
38. Team overnight accommodations
39. Pass leading to a basket
41. Sprains, twists and pulls
44. Stadium
45. Column heading on stat sheet (init.)
46. Grabbing
52. Reggie Slater's alma mater (init.)
53. Try (abbr.)
55. Raptors' conference
57. Turns sharply
59. Dine
63. Against (abbr.)
64. Column heading on roster (abbr.)

Solution on page 188

RETIRED UNIFORM NUMBERS

None

```
O  E  N  O  S  T  R  E  B  O  R  E  L  D  E
A  C  A  N  C  A  M  B  Y  K  S  B  W  R  R
N  H  O  R  I  M  Y  E  N  K  C  N  I  P  O
D  S  A  L  L  E  Y  A  R  R  U  M  L  O  W
E  I  D  S  E  F  D  S  L  O  A  K  L  R  E
R  S  A  N  I  U  I  O  N  D  I  U  I  R  R
S  Y  M  A  T  W  R  E  U  N  U  G  A  O  V
O  I  D  A  S  M  E  O  G  S  H  S  M  Z  S
N  E  B  A  I  O  T  L  G  T  I  E  S  I  Y
N  A  E  A  R  S  R  L  A  W  M  N  S  E  N
K  A  U  I  H  G  A  E  Z  A  D  O  R  R  B
S  M  D  L  C  A  C  O  K  A  G  L  E  O  T
S  B  R  E  L  L  I  M  V  L  V  A  G  M  Y
A  Y  H  I  J  A  P  I  T  S  A  M  O  H  T
M  U  J  O  N  E  S  L  E  F  F  W  R  S  A
```

ANDERSON	LEWIS	ROZIER
CAMBY	MALONE	SALLEY
CARTER	MCGRADY	STOUDAMIRE
CHRISTIE	MILLER	TABAK
DAVIS	MURRAY	THOMAS
EARL	PINCKNEY	WALKER
JONES	ROBERTSON	WILLIAMS
KING	ROGERS	WRIGHT

UTAH JAZZ

You could say that Pete Maravich was the original Jazz. But "Pistol Pete" became a player before the franchise even had a nickname. Or team colors. Or a coach for that matter.

It was Mar. 7, 1974, when New Orleans was granted an NBA franchise. A nine-man group paid $6.15 million for the expansion team. Less than two months later, the owners were sending four future draft choices to the Atlanta Hawks for Maravich.

It wasn't until then that the team nickname was chosen. It's surprising that it wasn't "Pistols."

The Jazz added 15 players through the expansion draft and Aaron James of Grambling in the college draft. That's when Scotty Robertson was named the first head coach.

New Orleans opened its inaugural season with a loss to the New York Knicks, 89–74. Maravich was the leading scorer with 15 points. The Jazz lost their first 11 games before finally beating the Portland Trail Blazers. When the Jazz's record hit 1–14, Robertson was replaced, first by Assistant Coach Elgin Baylor, then by Bill van Breda Kolff. They finished the season 24–59.

In 1975–76, the Jazz improved to 38–44, but van Breda Kolff was out, even when New Orleans got off to a 14–12 start the following season. Baylor was again the replacement. The Jazz went 35–47 and Maravich proved his worth. He led the NBA in scoring with 31.1 points a game, including 68 in one game vs. the Knicks.

The Jazz continued to struggle the next two years. Things were so bad they even resorted to a publicity stunt and selected a woman (Lucy Harris of nearby Delta State) in the 1977 college draft. Attendance began to slip.

Majority ownership was transferred to Sam Battisone and Larry Hatfield. Battisone owned the first Sambos restaurant outside of California and expanded from there. Hatfield was in the computer business as early as 1961 and his company was the first from the state of Mississippi to be listed on a national stock exchange. That pair moved the Jazz to Salt Lake City in the summer of 1979. It also was that summer when they acquired Adrian Dantley from the Los Angeles Lakers in exchange for Spencer Haywood. Tom Nissalke took over as head coach for the first season in Utah. By mid-season, Maravich had enough losing. He wanted to play for a winning team before his playing days were over. The club allowed Maravich to buy himself out of his contract and waived him. He then signed with the Boston Celtics.

In the spring of 1980, the Jazz lost the coin-flip for the No. 1 draft choice, but selected Louisville's Darrell Griffith with the second pick. He went on to win Rookie of the Year honors in the 1980–81 season. Dantley also reached his peak at the same time and led the league in scoring with 30.7 points per game. Yet, the Jazz still finished 28–54.

Nissalke was gone 20 games into the 1981–82 season, and he was replaced on the bench by general manager Frank Layden. The NBA funnyman and the fans laughed the rest of the way through a 25–57 season. In the 1982 college draft, the Jazz selected Georgia's Dominique Wilkins, but traded him before the start of the season to Atlanta for John Drew, Freeman Williams and cash. Even without 'Nique, Utah improved by 20 wins, going 45–37, and qualified for its first NBA playoffs. Layden was named the NBA Coach of the Year and the NBA Executive of the Year.

The Jazz began to pick up some good young players in the draft. They got Thurl Bailey and Bob Hansen in 1983, John Stockton in 1984 and Karl Malone in 1985. Utah never was able to get more than 47 wins under Layden, but it did make the playoffs in each of his five seasons. Finally, in 1988–89, Layden returned to the front office and named Jerry Sloan the head coach.

The Jazz won 51 games in Sloan's first year. That was the first of four straight 50+ win seasons. Malone and Stockton became perennial all-stars and both were named to the 1992 U.S. Olympic team. Stockton broke assist record after assist record and Malone broke other people's bones and backboards. It was the best 1–2 punch in the NBA.

The Jazz won a club-record 55 games in 1989–90, but were beaten in the first round of the playoffs by the Phoenix Suns. They won 54 games in 1990–91, but were beaten by the Portland Trail Blazers in the Conference semifinals. They won 55 games again in 1991–92 and advanced to the Western Conference finals before losing to Portland, 4 games to 2.

Utah slipped to a 47–35 record in 1992–93 and were eliminated by the Seattle SuperSonics in the first round of the playoffs. The Jazz rebounded to 53–29 in 1993–94 before losing to Houston in the Conference finals. They broke their own club record with 60 wins in 1994–95, but were upset by Houston in the opening round of the playoffs. And in 1995–96, the Jazz went 55–27 and advanced to the Conference finals before losing to Seattle.

The fans, media and club personnel were growing weary of not winning the NBA title. But first, the team had to get to the NBA Finals. In 1996–97, the Jazz finished 64–18, led by Malone who earned the NBA's MVP award. His dominance continued in the playoffs as Utah beat the L.A. Clippers, 3–0, the L.A. Lakers, 4–1, and then Houston, 4–2, to advance to the Finals for the first time. However, the Jazz faced the Chicago Bulls, coming off a 69-win season and defending their NBA title. The series was tied at two games apiece when the Bulls beat the Jazz in Salt Lake City, 90–88. The Bulls returned to Chicago and won the title in Game 6, 90–86.

The following year, the Jazz rolled to the NBA's best record, 62–20. They also swept the regular-season two-game series with the Bulls. The Jazz beat Houston, San Antonio and the L.A. Lakers in the playoffs to advance to the Finals. They again faced the Bulls, seeking their third consecutive title. Despite Utah's home court advantage, the Bulls again won in six games.

Copyright © 1998 Brian Spurlock/Spurlock Photography, Inc.

Karl Malone has scored 2,000+ points in 11 straight seasons, an NBA record.

INDIVIDUAL RECORDS

Career

Points: 27,782, Karl Malone, 1985–98

Rebounds: 11,376, Karl Malone, 1985–98

Assists: 12,713, John Stockton, 1984–98

Field Goal Pct.: .562, Adrian Dantley, 1979–86

Free Throw Pct.: .881, Jeff Malone, 1990–94

Season

Points: 2,540, Karl Malone, 1989–90

Rebounds: 1,288, Len Robinson, 1977–78

Assists: 1,164, John Stockton, 1990–91

Field Goal Pct.: .577, Adam Keefe, 1994–95

Free Throw Pct.: .917, Jeff Malone, 1990–91

ACROSS

2. Pistol Pete
6. Take a breather
9. Stadium
10. Basket
12. Bounce the ball
13. NBA's career assists leader
15. Rejection (init.)
16. Column heading on roster (abbr.)
17. Prep teammate of Darnell Valentine at Wichita Heights, Kan.
18. Roster spot for hurt players (init.)
19. Illegal defense
20. Grasp
23. Washington guard Sweets played 2 years in New Orleans
24. Jazz' career FG pct. leader
28. Away
29. ___ Meriweather
31. Direct
33. Stanford 7-footer played 5 years in N.O. and 2 in Utah
37. Carom at own basket (init.)
38. Arena sign
39. Hoop
41. Jazz' starting point guard before Stockton
43. Coach: ___ way or the highway!

44. Mode of team travel

45. Ahead: ___ top

46. Jazz' head coach in final year at New Orleans

48. A cheer

50. Dream Team: Team ___

52. No game today

54. Leg joint

55. Number of seconds allowed to cross center line

57. Part of FGA

58. Dines

59. Assist

61. Painted stripes

62. Back-up player

DOWN

1. Upper limb

2. Jazz' career scoring leader

3. Drive hard: Take it to the ___

4. Up and ___

5. Set Jazz record with 8 3-pointers in '94 game

7. Alley-oop passes

8. Every 7 days

9. Directs a shot

11. Truck

13. Jazz' head coach

14. ___-captain

15. Trick defense: ___-and-1

21. Jazz' 1st head coach

22. Wager on a game

25. Everyone

26. Jazz' resident jokester

27. Selection of college players

30. Basketball's minor league (init.)

32. End of a foot

34. Prep teammate of Jalen Rose and Voshon Lenard

35. Lower limb

36. Type of shot

39. Play-___-play announcer

40. Top of the ___

42. 1st year players

43. The Bear, Gorilla and Boomer

47. Try (abbr.)

49. Jumps

51. Positions on the low blocks

52. Game sphere

53. Former

56. Tidy

59. ___ shoots, he scores!

60. 1-pointer (init.)

Solution on page 189

RETIRED UNIFORM NUMBERS

1	Frank Layden
7	Pete Maravich
35	Darrell Griffith
53	Mark Eaton

P	K	S	Y	O	S	T	E	R	T	A	G	A	D	M
O	E	E	T	E	W	H	C	I	V	A	R	A	M	B
Q	L	K	P	O	L	O	L	A	S	O	N	L	R	H
U	L	R	O	I	C	S	J	L	R	T	O	O	U	T
E	E	I	N	A	Y	K	I	A	L	R	W	L	S	I
T	Y	S	D	R	A	W	D	E	M	N	W	A	S	F
T	E	L	O	L	E	N	Y	O	L	E	L	Y	E	F
E	N	Y	U	N	A	O	L	S	N	S	S	N	L	I
H	O	R	N	A	C	E	K	H	A	N	S	O	L	R
T	T	Y	O	R	L	E	C	M	E	A	O	T	N	G
I	K	O	E	O	I	I	E	D	T	H	U	A	O	P
K	C	T	I	R	O	L	Y	A	B	N	E	E	R	G
K	O	T	O	N	I	A	N	I	S	S	A	L	K	E
T	T	O	N	S	L	A	H	T	E	N	O	L	A	M
W	S	R	O	B	I	N	S	O	N	T	Q	U	E	N

BAYLOR	GRIFFITH	MCELROY
BROWN	HANSEN	NISSALKE
CARR	HORNACEK	OSTERTAG
DANTLEY	JAMES	POQUETTE
EATON	KELLEY	ROBINSON
EDWARDS	LAYDEN	RUSSELL
EISLEY	MALONE	SLOAN
GREEN	MARAVICH	STOCKTON

VANCOUVER GRIZZLIES

The city of Vancouver can thank Arthur Griffiths for having a team in the National Basketball Association today. For anyone living outside of British Columbia, the name Arthur Griffiths may not ring a bell. But inside the province, Griffiths' name is synonymous with professional sports and good-will. His family has owned the Vancouver Canucks in the National Hockey League for 28 years and Arthur remains on the NHL Board of Governors, along with the NBA's board.

Griffiths alerted the NBA on Feb. 24, 1993, that he was interested in securing a franchise. Five months later, the NBA's expansion committee made its official visit to Vancouver, but not until ground had been broken on the new General Motors Place arena.

On Feb. 12, 1994, the "Vancouver Mounties" had its bid unanimously endorsed by the expansion committee, and a conditional franchise was awarded two-and-a-half months later for $125 million.

Former NBA head coach Stu Jackson was named the vice president of basketball operations, July 22, 1994.

A short time later, the team's new nickname, Grizzlies, along with the logo and team colors were unveiled.

On June 1, 1995, the Grizzlies signed their first player: free agent guard Kevin Pritchard, a member of the 1988 NCAA champion Kansas Jayhawks. Then on June 19, Brian Winters, a veteran of 18 seasons in the NBA as a player and assistant coach, was named head coach. His assistants the first season were Rex Hughes, Lionel Hollins and Jim Powell.

The following week, Vancouver joined the other new team, the Toronto Raptors, in the expansion draft of veteran NBA players. The Grizzlies came away with 13 players: Greg Anthony (from the New York Knicks), Benoit Benjamin (New Jersey), Rodney Dent (Orlando), Blue Edwards (Utah), Doug Edwards (Atlanta), Kenny Gattison (Charlotte), Antonio Harvey (L.A. Lakers), Derrick Phelps (Sacramento), Trevor Ruffin (Phoenix), Byron Scott (Indiana), Reggie Slater (Denver), Larry Stewart (Washington) and Gerald Wilkins (Cleveland).

Then on June 28, 1995, the Grizzlies took part in the college draft. With the sixth overall pick in the first round, Vancouver selected Oklahoma State's Bryant "Big Country" Reeves. Lawrence Moten from Syracuse was the second-round pick (36th overall). Prior to the season, the Grizzlies signed free agents Chris King, Ashraf Amaya and Rich Manning, then unloaded their original signee—Pritchard—before he ever played a game. Vancouver sent Pritchard and Stewart to Orlando for forward Anthony Avent.

The Grizzlies opened their inaugural season at Portland, Nov. 3, 1995. Vancouver started Anthony, Blue Edwards, Benjamin, Gattison and King. It was King who scored the Grizzlies' first points, hitting a bucket 1:30 into the game. The Grizzlies stayed competitive the entire game, and won, 92–80. Benjamin led the team with 29 points and 13 rebounds. They debuted at home two days later and nipped Minnesota, 100–98, in overtime.

While local fans celebrated and had visions of championships, the Grizzlies were suddenly struck with a hammer labeled "reality." Vancouver lost its next 19 games. The NBA record for most consecutive losses in a season was 20, and when the Grizzlies took the floor at home against Portland, Dec. 15, they wanted to avoid getting their name in the records book that quickly. But Vancouver, led by Reeves' 25 points and 17 rebounds, beat the Trail Blazers in overtime.

The Grizzlies added losing streaks of six games and four games (twice), prior to a 93–86 victory over Sacramento on Valentine's Day to stand at 11–37. The Grizzlies didn't win again, though, until Apr. 3. Vancouver lost 23 games in a row to get the NBA record for futility that it worked so hard to avoid earlier in the season. The streak finally was snapped against Minnesota, 105–103. After losses in seven of their next eight games, the Grizzlies closed out the season with two straight wins on the road to finish 15–67, the worst record in the NBA and six victories behind national rival, Toronto. They were 10–31 at home and 5–36 on the road.

The Grizzlies used their No. 1 choice in the 1996 college draft to tab California's freshman forward, Shareef Abdur-Rahim, with the third overall selection. The Grizzlies used another first-round pick (the 22nd overall) to get Alabama forward Roy Rogers. In the second round, they chose swing man Chris Robinson from Western Kentucky.

The Grizzlies' didn't think things could get much worse than their first season. They were wrong. Vancouver started out 0–7 in 1996–97. It was 2–16, 3–19, 4–20, 5–22, 6–27, 7–32, then 8–35 when Winters was fired and replaced on the bench by Jackson. Additional losing streaks of 15 and 9 games compounded the problems. The Grizzlies won two of their final three games (both on the road) to finish 14–68.

Brian Hill was hired as the head coach prior to the 1997–98 season. The Grizzlies used the fourth overall pick in the draft to select Antonio Daniels from Bowling Green.

Abdur-Rahim averaged 22.3 points per game to lead five players in double-figures. The Grizzlies were much more competitive night in and night out and improved to 19–63. That was better than three teams, including Toronto (16 wins).

Vancouver used the second overall selection in the draft to obtain Mike Bibby from Arizona, then traded Daniels to San Antonio for Carl Herrera and the draft rights to Felipe Lopez.

Antonio Daniels averaged 4.5 assists per game as a rookie in 1997–98.

INDIVIDUAL RECORDS

Career

Points: 19,383, George Gervin, 1976–85

Rebounds: 7,389, David Robinson, 1989–98

Assists: 3,865, Johnny Moore, 1980–88, 1989–90

Field Goal Pct.: .620, Artis Gilmore, 1982–87

Free Throw Pct.: .861, Johnny Dawkins, 1986–89

Season

Points: 2,585, George Gervin, 1983–84

Rebounds: 1,367, Dennis Rodman, 1993–94

Assists: 816, Johnny Moore, 1984–85

Field Goal Pct.: .632, Steve Johnson, 1985–86

Free Throw Pct.: .896, Johnny Dawkins, 1987–88

ACROSS

6. Game sphere
9. Technical, personal and flagrant
11. Center chosen in expansion draft wore uniform number 00
12. Take the ball away (abbr.)
13. Wire service
14. Theodore Edwards' nickname
15. Man, zone or press
17. Anthony Peeler's alma mater (init.)
21. Benoit Benjamin's alma mater (init.)
22. Set Grizzlies' record with 1,829 points in 1997–98
26. Kept on the scoreboard (abbr.)
28. Play-___-play announcer
29. Nick Anderson's alma mater (init.)
30. Roster spot for hurt players (init.)
31. Pain
32. Alabama teammate of Antonio McDyess and Jason Caffey
34. Season
35. Special guest (init.)
36. Blue
37. Play ___ or trade me!
38. Where severely injured players are sent (init.)
40. Go head first onto the floor
41. 1st sound at press conference for nervous rookie

43. Throw the ball away (abbr.)
44. Former Laker great chosen in expansion draft
45. Ashraf
47. Arena sign
49. Remaining
50. Secretarial pool
52. Point value of FT
54. Music disk (init.)
55. Scorches
56. Grizzlies' head coach
57. Deadlocks
58. Michigan team: ___ Five
60. Dream Team: Team ___
61. High school player
64. ___-captain
65. Column heading on roster (abbr.)
66. Knee or elbow protection
67. Pass leading to a basket (abbr.)
68. Hangs from the middle of the roof

DOWN

1. ___ or die
2. Aide (abbr.)
3. Vegetarian guard was 1st round pick of the Lakers in '92
4. Slam
5. Painted stripe
7. Stadium
8. Get beat
9. Team operation granted by NBA
10. Rich Manning's alma mater (init.)

16. 1-pointer (init.)
18. Arkansas guard signed with Grizzlies after 4 years in Milwaukee
19. Set Grizzlies' season record by making 83.7% of his FT in 1997–98
20. 14-year veteran traded to Sacramento during 1997–98 season
23. 1st college player drafted by the Grizzlies
24. Media guide photos
25. Providence guard acquired from Milwaukee in '95
26. Cuonzo Martin's alma mater (init.)
27. Kept on the scoreboard
33. Dines
37. Syracuse guard chosen in the 2nd round of the '95 draft
39. Basket
42. Game official
45. Grizzlies' career assists leader
46. Stomach muscle (abbr.)
47. Away
48. Guards
49. Alley-oop pass
51. Utilize
52. Points ___ turnovers
53. Arm joint
54. Teams
57. Tip
59. ___ Green (init.)
61. Paid player
62. Corner bar
63. Whirlpool

Solution on page 189

RETIRED UNIFORM NUMBERS

None

```
Y  N  O  A  M  A  Y  A  R  E  L  E  E  P  W
Y  R  O  B  I  N  S  O  N  N  M  R  D  W  M
T  U  R  D  E  S  M  A  I  L  L  I  W  B  A
U  R  W  U  A  N  I  T  R  A  M  Y  A  E  Y
M  M  U  R  D  O  C  K  L  U  A  O  R  N  B
I  O  I  R  Y  Y  H  E  T  Y  N  F  D  J  E
H  T  S  A  V  E  N  T  B  T  N  L  S  A  R
A  E  U  H  Z  L  E  Y  J  T  I  C  E  M  R
R  N  U  I  B  B  N  N  H  U  N  G  H  I  Y
S  M  Z  M  E  O  K  I  J  C  G  N  N  S
E  X  C  E  H  M  L  B  V  L  I  N  B  E  P
V  Y  N  T  H  L  N  A  Z  I  M  Y  I  W  M
E  S  N  R  O  G  E  R  S  H  I  I  P  K  O
E  A  T  T  O  C  S  J  A  C  K  S  O  N  H
R  W  I  N  T  E  R  S  I  T  X  Y  N  S  T
```

ABDUR-RAHIM	JACKSON	MURDOCK
AMAYA	KING	PEELER
ANTHONY	LYNCH	REEVES
AVENT	MANNING	ROBINSON
BENJAMIN	MARTIN	ROGERS
CHILCUTT	MAYBERRY	SCOTT
EDWARDS	MOBLEY	WILLIAMS
HILL	MOTEN	WINTERS

WASHINGTON WIZARDS

Even though the 1989 induction ceremonies for the Naismith Memorial Basketball Hall of Fame were held in Springfield, Mass., there was more interest in Washington, D.C., than any other place in the nation. Of the four players inducted that year, three of them were former Bullets. According to the Hall of Fame, that's the only time that three members of the same franchise were inducted in the same year.

Elvin Hayes, Earl Monroe and Dave Bing were honored in Springfield that day, but the memories of their exploits will remain in the minds of Bullets fans for a long time to come.

Hayes played nine years for the Bullets, was named to the all-star team eight times and was the club's leading scorer seven times. Monroe was a Bullet for five years. He was the NBA Rookie of the Year, a two-time all-star and led the team in scoring four times. And Bing played for the Bullets two years, leading the team in assists one season.

That trio was instrumental in the Bullets' success in the 1970s, but another man who had been inducted into the Hall of Fame two years earlier, was just as important. Wes Unseld, a 6-foot-7, 245-pound muscle man out of Louisville, crashed the boards and set picks for 13 seasons as a Bullet. For the past five-and-a-half years, Unseld has served as the club's head coach.

Unseld was the second player selected in the 1968 college draft. He was runner-up to no one for a long time after that. Not only did he win the NBA Rookie of the Year award, but was also the league MVP the same season. He averaged 13.8 points (fewest of any MVP winner) and 18.2 rebounds a game. But more importantly, he helped the Bullets improve from 36 wins the previous season to a league-high 57 in 1968–69.

That was the start of an 11-year span when the Bullets were one of the most successful franchises in the league. Over that period, they won their division seven times, finished second three times and third once. They won the NBA title in 1977–78 and reached the Finals two other times. What is most impressive, though, is that they accomplished that under three different coaches and a number of different line-ups.

The foundation of their success goes back to the beginning of the team. It originated in 1961–62 as the expansion Chicago Packers. They became known as the Chicago Zephyrs the following year. When they were unable to get an acceptable arena deal, they moved to Baltimore where a brand new downtown arena waited. The name was changed to the Bullets. Then in 1964, the club was sold to a group headed by Abe Pollin for a then-record $1.1 million. Pollin remains the owner today.

The franchise slowly improved on the floor in each of its first five years, but in 1966–67 it slipped to a 20–61 record. The Bullets went through three coaches that season, but the third one, Gene Shue, stayed for a six-and-a-half year stint. That record did enable the Bullets, however, to select second in the 1967 college draft. They chose Monroe out of tiny Winston-Salem. "Earl the Pearl" was an instant success. He averaged 24.3 points a game. The Bullets improved to 36 wins, but they still wound up sixth in their division and with the second overall pick in the draft again.

This time they got Unseld and the turnaround continued. The 57 wins in 1968–69 were followed by 50, then a run of five straight division titles. In the summer of 1972 the Bullets became even stronger when they acquired Hayes from the Houston Rockets for Jack Marin and future considerations.

In the summer of 1973, the Bullets moved to Washington and planned to be tenants in someone else's building. But those plans fell through and Pollin built his own arena. But not just any arena would do. The Capital Centre was the first in the U.S. with large, luxury sky boxes, the first with a four-sided instant replay screen and the first with fully computerized ticketing. The Bullets also hired a new coach, K.C. Jones. They were known as the Capital Bullets for one year before changing their name to the Washington Bullets beginning with the 1974–75 season.

The Bullets recorded the best record in the league in 1974–75 and advanced to the NBA Finals before losing to the Golden State Warriors, 4 games to none. The Bullets were in the Finals again in 1977–78, this time under Coach Dick Motta. The Bullets overcame a 3 games to 2 deficit and upset the SuperSonics at Seattle in the deciding Game 7. The following season the same teams met in the Finals again and the Sonics won this time, 4–1.

Since then Washington has been unable to find the same success. It has averaged 36 wins a year with no more than 44 in any season and stumbled to four straight sub-26-win seasons from 1991–92 to 1994–95. Washington rebounded slightly in 1995–96, behind Juwan Howard and Chris Webber, and finished 39–43. But that marked the eighth straight season without a playoff berth, the longest streak in the league at that time.

In 1996–97, with a coaching change that saw Jim Lynam depart and Bernie Bickerstaff enter at mid-season, Washington finished 44–38 and made the playoffs. Despite elimination in the first round (a 3–0 sweep by eventual champion Chicago), excitement in the Capital City was high.

The team changed its name again for the 1997–98 season—to the Washington Wizards. There were new team colors and new uniforms. And to top it off, there was a new arena—the MCI Center—in downtown Washington.

The Wizards finished 42–40, but off-the-court problems caused G.M. Unseld to begin breaking up the nucleus of the team.

Juwan Howard was a member of the University of Michigan's "Fab Five."

INDIVIDUAL RECORDS

Career

        Points: 15,551, Elvin Hayes, 1972–81

        Rebounds: 13,769, Wes Unseld, 1968–81

        Assists: 3,822, Wes Unseld, 1968–81

        Field Goal Pct.: .578, Gheorghe Muresan, 1993–97

        Free Throw Pct.: .869, Jeff Malone, 1983–90

Season

        Points: 2,495, Walt Bellamy, 1961–62

        Rebounds: 1,500, Walt Bellamy, 1961–62

        Assists: 801, Rod Strickland, 1997–98

        Field Goal Pct.: .604, Gheorghe Muresan, 1996–97

        Free Throw Pct.: .894, Jack Marin, 1971–72

ACROSS

1. Teams
4. NBA MVP as a rookie in 1968–69
10. Smack
13. Elvin Hayes' alma mater (init.)
14. Carom at own basket (init.)
15. Fruit drink
17. Point value of FG
20. Logo registration (abbr.)
22. Wizards' head coach
24. Possible college major for jocks (init.)
25. Bonzi Wells' alma mater (init.)
26. Former

27. Michigan team: ___ Five
28. West Coast rival (init.)
30. Painted stripe
31. Calbert Cheaney's alma mater (init.)
32. Boo-boo
33. Wizards' home district (init.)
35. Set team record with 24 assists in '80 game
37. Dudley Bradley's alma mater (init.)
40. Boast
41. Tap
43. Wizards' career leader in 3-pointers
45. Juwan

46. Away
48. 1-pointers
50. Basketball's minor league (init.)
51. Column heading on roster (abbr.)
52. Set team record with 2,495 points in 1961–62
55. Basket cord
58. Wes Unseld's alma mater (init.)
59. Total assists divided by games played
62. Big Gheorghe
63. Fastbreak
65. California guard was 1st round pick in '71 and remains as TV announcer
66. Knee protection
67. The paint
68. Ref's relative

DOWN

2. Allow
3. Sound of displeasure from fan
5. Nick Mantis' alma mater (init.)
6. Head coach, 1980–86, and family
7. Alley-oop passes
8. Team physician (abbr.)
9. Unsigned player (init.)
10. ___ shoots, he scores!
11. Break in play
12. Type of x ray (init.)
16. Guard
18. Part of 27 Across

19. Wizards' career scoring leader
20. Last column on box score (init.)
21. Points ___ turnovers
22. Team's former nickname
23. ___-captain
29. Earl the Pearl
30. Head coach, 1986–87
34. Turn sharply
36. Weird
38. Lacking bravery
39. Set club record with 801 assists in 1997–98
42. Guard, forward and center
43. At
44. Direct a shot
47. Sixers star ___ Greer
48. Spectators
49. Play ___ or trade me!
53. In 8 NBA seasons guard has played for Washington, Golden St., Dallas, Utah, Denver and Phoenix
54. Arena sign
56. Jerry Sloan's alma mater (init.)
57. Attempt
58. ___ vs. Them
60. Against (abbr.)
61. Sprint
62. Greet
63. Basket
64. Roster spot for hurt players (init.)
66. ___-announcer (init.)

Solution on page 190

RETIRED UNIFORM NUMBERS

11	Elvin Hayes
25	Gus Johnson
41	Wes Unseld

```
A F F A T S R E K C I B H S E
B Y O K N O N O S N H O J U K
D Y E V E R G M N U W O H I G
N A O L L K S T W A N S N R N
A L O N I O N E R E T R O P E
L L I N R A B D S O T V I C D
U H G J R E I N E H C N L H N
R L A G E U E R E Y H A A E A
O E A Y E O R N O M D T A A L
D S B L E R A M O A N T T N K
L N I B E S A O M L L O T E C
E U R E E R N S O E A M H Y I
S B A R I W R Y A R R U M C R
N N U N M B E L L A M Y O L T
U M A L O N E R E N N A R A S
```

ADAMS

BELLAMY

BICKERSTAFF

CHEANEY

CHENIER

GRANT

GREVEY

HAYES

HOWARD

JOHNSON

JONES

KING

MALONE

MARIN

MONROE

MOTTA

MURESAN

MURRAY

PORTER

RULAND

SHUE

STRICKLAND

UNSELD

WEBBER

CROSSWORD SOLUTIONS

ATLANTA HAWKS

BOSTON CELTICS

CHARLOTTE HORNETS

CHICAGO BULLS

CLEVELAND CAVALIERS

DALLAS MAVERICKS

DENVER NUGGETS

DETROIT PISTONS

GOLDEN STATE WARRIORS

HOUSTON ROCKETS

INDIANA PACERS

LOS ANGELES CLIPPERS

LOS ANGELES LAKERS

MIAMI HEAT

MILWAUKEE BUCKS

MINNESOTA TIMBERWOLVES

NEW JERSEY NETS

NEW YORK KNICKS

ORLANDO MAGIC

PHILADELPHIA 76ERS

PHOENIX SUNS

PORTLAND TRAIL BLAZERS

SACRAMENTO KINGS

SAN ANTONIO SPURS

SEATTLE SUPERSONICS

TORONTO RAPTORS

UTAH JAZZ

VANCOUVER GRIZZLIES

WASHINGTON WIZARDS